Crone
Health and Safety

Written and compiled by the staff of
Croner's Employment Law and Human Resources
Editorial Department

Revised and updated by
Mike Murray
Consultant

Croner Publications Ltd
Croner House
London Road
Kingston upon Thames
Surrey KT2 6SR
Telephone: 0181-547 3333

First edition October 1987
Second edition April 1991
Third edition November 1995
Fourth edition May 1998

Published by
Croner Publications Ltd
Croner House
London Road
Kingston upon Thames
Surrey KT2 6SR
Telephone: 0181-547 3333

While every care has been taken in the writing and editing of this book, readers should be aware that only Acts of Parliament and Statutory Instruments have the force of law and that only the courts can authoritatively interpret the law.

British Library Cataloguing-in-Publication Data
Croner's guide to health and safety.
Croner's Employment Law Editorial Department
658.3

ISBN 1 85524 461 6

Typeset by Letterpart Ltd
Printed by Clays Ltd, St Ives plc

Contents

Introduction

This book is not intended to serve as a complete guide to the law on health and safety at work. Its main purpose is to give managers and those people running their own small businesses assistance in the practical implementation of the law in accordance with their own organisation's health and safety policies. In this context, "manager" means any person with responsibility for supervising the work performance of another employee. Health and safety should be a factor for consideration at all levels in an organisation. Accordingly the book concentrates on issues such as accidents, recognised union-appointed safety representatives and health problems. However, specific legal issues are covered briefly within each chapter whenever appropriate.

The book also gives guidance on the unfair dismissal provisions relating to health and safety at work. It must be emphasised, however, that the guidance and recommendations contained in this book are general in nature. It is essential that they are read in conjunction with the employer's policies and procedures.

1 The Legislation

Until the mid-1970s, the law relating to health and safety at work was primarily contained in the **Factories Act 1961**, the **Offices, Shops and Railway Premises Act 1963** and associated regulations. There were also a number of disparate pieces of legislation applying to specific activities. These Acts and regulations were (and the parts which remain still are) very prescriptive, setting out detailed requirements which must be met. However, they applied only to specific places of work and/or activities, leaving many others without any health and safety controls whatsoever. This unsatisfactory situation changed completely with the passing of the **Health and Safety at Work, etc Act 1974**. The Act represented a whole new approach to health and safety law in that, for the first time ever, it imposed general obligations on all those concerned with health, safety and welfare at work — manufacturers, suppliers and employees as well as employers.

Despite the many legislative changes which have taken place since 1974, the general duties laid down by the **Health and Safety at Work, etc Act 1974** still form the basis of health and safety regulation in the UK. In many areas, however, the means by which those duties must be fulfilled has now become the subject of more detailed regulation. In most cases, this has happened in response to the requirements of European law.

The Effect of the European Union

European law, which has had an enormous impact on UK health and safety legislation in recent years, could be seen as a move back to a more prescriptive approach. The majority of EU legislation on health and safety is enacted by means of directives. A directive sets out the standards that must be achieved by Member States but leaves the means of enactiment to the individual states. In the UK such directives are normally implemented by regulations made under the **Health and Safety at Work, etc Act 1974**.

The major initiative of the EU was the adoption of the Framework Directive (Directive 89/931), which is concerned with the introduction of measures to encourage improvements in the health and safety of workers at work. This directive covers all workplaces and is concerned with general health and safety principles. Under its provisions, "daughter" directives can be enacted to cover particular workplaces or situations. In 1993, the UK incorporated the Framework Directive into its health and safety legislation by means of the **Management of Health and Safety at Work Regulations 1992**. In that same year, five other sets of regulations were introduced to implement various "daughter" directives. These covered display screen equipment, work equipment, workplace health and safety, manual handling and personal protective equipment. Since then a number of other daughter directives have been enacted into UK legislation, covering such areas as biological agents, protection of young workers and the protection of pregnant workers. In general, these have been incorporated by means of amending existing legislation.

The Factories Act 1961 and the Offices, Shops and Railway Premises Act 1963

The **Factories Act 1961** covered (and in some cases still covers) three main areas — general health and welfare provisions, general safety provisions and certain measures relating to young people, ie those below 18 years of age.

The health and welfare aspects of the Act covered cleanliness of the factory, overcrowding, minimum temperatures, ventilation, drainage, lighting, drinking water, washing facilities, accommodation for clothing and seating.

The safety provisions governed hoists and lifts, chains, ropes and lifting tackle, cranes and other lifting machines, floors, passages and stairs, the fencing, guarding and cleaning of machinery, safe means of access, safe places of employment, dangerous or explosive substances or fumes, steam boilers, receivers and containers, air receivers and gasholders. There were also certain provisions relating to particular substances and processes.

The **Offices, Shops and Railway Premises Act 1963** governed many of the same areas of health and safety as the **Factories Act 1961**, although standards were not identical. To a large extent, the provisions of these two Acts have now been superseded by more recent legislation, but in some cases they continue to apply until the new provisions are completely in place. Details (including transitional arrangements) are provided under various subject headings throughout this book.

The Health and Safety at Work, etc Act 1974

The term "so far as is reasonably practicable" recurs throughout the **Health and Safety at Work, etc Act 1974**. In broad terms this involves balancing the degree of risk to employees against money, time or trouble involved in minimising the risk. If the likelihood of injury is insignificant and it would be very expensive to take precautions, such precautions are likely to be deemed not reasonably practicable.

For the purposes of this book the following are the main duties imposed by the Act.

Employers' Duties

Employers are under a general duty to ensure, so far as is reasonably practicable, the health, safety and welfare at work of all their employees. This includes:

- the provision and maintenance of plant and systems of work that are safe and without risks to health
- arrangements for ensuring safety and absence of risks to health in connection with the use, handling, storage and transport of articles and substances
- the provision of such information, instruction, training and supervision as is necessary to ensure the health and safety at work of their employees
- the maintenance of any place of work under their control, in a condition that is safe and without risks to health, and the provision and maintenance of means of access to and egress from the place of work that are safe and without such risks
- the provision and maintenance of a working environment for employees which is safe, without risks to health and adequate with regard to facilities and arrangements for their welfare at work.

Employees' Duties

All employees are under a duty to take reasonable care for the health and safety at work of themselves and any other people who might be affected by their acts or omissions and to co-operate with their employers and others to enable them to comply with statutory duties and requirements.

Additionally, they must not intentionally or recklessly misuse anything provided in the interests of health, safety or welfare in pursuance of any aspect of health and safety law.

Manufacturers', Designers', Importers' and Suppliers' Duties

Manufacturers, designers, importers and suppliers must:

- ensure, so far as is reasonably practicable, that articles are designed and constructed in such a manner as to be safe and without risks to health when being set, used, cleaned or maintained or stored in "reasonably foreseeable circumstances"
- ensure, so far as is reasonably practicable, that substances are safe and without risks to health when being used, handled, processed, stored or transported
- ensure that necessary tests and examinations are carried out
- provide adequate information about the uses, tests and any conditions which must be observed in the use of articles or substances.

Other Provisions

The Act also requires employers who employ at least five employees to prepare written policy statements (see page 35) and where requested to provide for the appointment of safety representatives and safety committees (see pages 24 and 32).

In addition, the general provisions of the Act impose specific responsibilities on those to whom the Act applies.

The Management of Health and Safety at Work Regulations 1992

The **Management of Health and Safety at Work Regulations 1992** came into force on 1 January 1993 and were amended in 1994. They apply to all workplaces and to all employees (also to the self-employed and employees of a third party).

Risk Assessment

At the heart of the regulations is the requirement for employers to assess what health and safety risks their employees (and others) may be exposed to as a result of their work. Having made the assessment, the employer must then decide what steps he or she is going to take in order to protect those concerned by complying with relevant health and safety legislation. Where five or more workers are employed, the employer must record:

- the findings of the risk assessment, and
- the measures taken to control the risks identified.

(See page 10.)

"Competent" Persons

Under the regulations, employers are required to appoint one or more "competent" persons to help them identify risks and find solutions. These will be people with enough training and experience to enable them to assist the employer properly in a particular area. A manager may well be the competent person or be called upon to help the competent person. However, the competent person need not necessarily be an employee of the company and, for example, may be an appropriately qualified consultant.

Health Surveillance

In some work situations, there may be a risk of particular health problems or diseases developing. Where this is the case then health surveillance (and keeping health records for each individual) will be necessary.

Emergency Procedures

Under the regulations, employers must set up procedures to be followed in the event of serious and imminent danger. There must be sufficient "competent" people nominated to implement those procedures should the need arise.

Information and Training

Employees must be informed about any health and safety risks that have been identified and must be told what preventive steps are being taken to protect them. They must also be given adequate and suitable health and safety training.

Employees' Duties

It is worth noting that the regulations also impose a duty on employees to follow health and safety instructions, and to report to the employer any dangerous situations in the workplace or any shortcomings in health and safety arrangements.

Risk Assessment

Aim

The purpose of risk assessment is to identify the hazards and risks associated with a particular workplace or activity and the steps that need to be taken to protect workers from them such that an employer may fulfil his or her obligations under the relevant legislation.

Assessment

The assessment should:

- be "suitable" and "sufficient"
- be carried out by a "competent" person, and
- enable the employer to set the organisation's health and safety priorities.

Definitions

"Hazard" is anything which can cause harm. "Risk" is the chance that any particular hazard *will* cause harm.

Identifying Hazards

Hazards in the workplace come in all shapes and sizes. Examples include lifting heavy loads, using machinery, working at height and exposure to loud noise. Many hazards may be readily identified by simply walking around the workplace and making careful observations. However, it is also a good idea to go and ask those who are doing the work for their views, since they will know — probably better than anyone else — what the problems are. The accident book will be a useful source of information, especially when comparisons are made with national and/or industry statistics.

Evaluating Risks

Once the risks have been identified, they must be evaluated and put into order of importance. The simplest way is to attach some sort of rating to each risk, such as high, medium or low, although in some situations a more complex system will be called for.

Reducing Risks

The employer will need to decide whether existing precautions are adequate or whether more should be done. Appropriate measures might include substituting the activity by a less hazardous one or reducing the number of people exposed to the hazard.

Record and Review

The findings of the risk assessment should be recorded, and should be reviewed from time to time to ensure that they remain valid.

Informing Employees about Health and Safety

Employers are required to bring to the attention of their employees certain information about health and safety law and to provide them with the local addresses of the authorities which enforce that law. In order to do this, they may either display an approved poster in the workplace or supply their employees with an approved leaflet. Both poster and leaflet are produced by the Health and Safety Executive (HSE) and are available from branches of The Stationery Office.

Where the leaflet system is used, every employee must be given a copy together with the local addresses of the relevant enforcing authority and the HSE's Employment Medical Advisory Service (EMAS).

Where the poster is used, it must be situated in a readily accessible and visible position and must always be kept in a good readable condition. The addresses of the relevant enforcing authority and EMAS office must be completed in the spaces provided on the poster.

In addition to the above, those engaged in particular industries and processes must also display the relevant regulations which apply to them.

Further Advice

Advice and information on health and safety legislation and general safety matters may be obtained from the HSE. Addresses and telephone numbers of their offices are given in the Appendix. Information on medical matters may be obtained from the EMAS. Medical advisors are located at the addresses given in the Appendix.

2 Accidents at Work

It is a vital part of the manager's job to help prevent, or at the very least minimise, accidents at work. However, despite the best endeavours of employers, accidents at work will continue to occur and it is therefore important that managers are aware of their responsibilities. Essentially there are three vital roles which will have to be undertaken: attending to the accident victim, managing the rest of the department, and the legal implications.

While many companies operate formal procedures governing such matters (perhaps involving passing responsibility for the injured employee to the personnel department and calling on the company's legal service), it is important that the manager, as the person on the spot, understands what has to be done so that the company copes with the accident as humanely and effectively as possible.

The Injured Employee

Obviously the manager's first concern must be for the employee who has suffered the accident. A quick visual check should ascertain whether the company first aider should be summoned or whether it is more sensible to dial 999 immediately.

If the victim is unconscious or has possibly broken a bone, no attempt should be made to move him or her unless it is necessary to guard against further injury. Untold damage can be caused by kindly attempts to make people more comfortable.

Having called in the appropriate "expert" the most important task, so far as the injured person is concerned, is to provide the most comfort and support possible. In the case of "the walking wounded", they should be taken to a comfortable and, if possible, private place to await medical attention. This achieves two things at once. It removes an upsetting and disruptive spectacle from other employees, and allows the injured person to suffer in peace and quiet. Similarly, no one likes having witnesses to his or her reaction to pain and suffering.

If the injured person has to go to hospital it is important that the manager or another responsible person goes with them. If a hospital stay is required there will be a multitude of things to do. The most important of these is notifying the person's next of kin. While this is a task that the police will undertake, it should be done, if at all possible, by a responsible person who has all the necessary details: how the accident happened, the condition of the employee, and the name, telephone number and location of the hospital. Above all it is essential that this person has the ability to impart this information clearly but with great sensitivity, particularly in the case of a serious injury.

The more the organisation shows itself willing to smooth out the problems consequent on a sudden admission to hospital, the less likely it is that there will be other disruption to the business activities in terms of the attitudes of the victim's colleagues and the length of his or her recovery time and date of return to work.

Managing the Department

With so much attention being paid to the victim, other members of the department must not be forgotten. It is important that, as far as possible, normal work is resumed as quickly as practicable. This is not as heartless as it might sound. Witnessing an accident can be an extremely traumatic event and if appearances of normality are restored quickly and people are occupied with their daily routine, the shock may be lessened. However, there may be some employees, particularly those who were working next to or are on close terms with the victim of a serious accident, who are too shocked to continue working. Sending them straight home could lead to them having an accident if they drive, or returning to an empty house to brood on events. It is usually better to ensure that they are taken to a quiet area, and given the opportunity to talk about the accident.

One essential task for the manager, or for someone such as the works manager or safety manager, is obviously to determine whether the circumstances of the accident make it possible that a machine was at fault, in which case all similar machines will need to be shut down until they have been examined thoroughly. If the accident was due to a spillage it must be cleaned up properly. If it is decided that normal working can be safely resumed, the reasons for this decision should be explained to the workforce in order to allay any fears they may have for their own safety.

There will inevitably be other action required by managers as a result of the accident and this is dealt with under *Follow-up Procedures* (see page 19).

The Legal Issues

There are three potential legal areas which must be borne in mind when an employee has an accident at work: the **Reporting of Injuries, Diseases and Dangerous Occurrences Regulations 1995** may apply; the employee may take out a civil action against the employer for damages; the employer, or other employees, may be prosecuted under the **Health and Safety at Work, etc Act 1974**.

The Reporting Regulations

Certain accidents must be reported to the enforcement authority (either the Health and Safety Executive (HSE) or local authority), either immediately or within 10 days (see page 16).

Major Injury Accidents

- all fractures except to fingers, thumbs or toes
- all amputations
- the loss of sight of an eye, a penetrating injury to the eye, or a chemical or hot metal burn to the eye
- either injury (including burns) requiring immediate medical treatment or loss of consciousness, resulting in either case from an electric shock from any electrical circuit or equipment, whether or not due to direct contact (this therefore includes cases where a person is injured by arcing or flashover without actually touching live equipment)
- loss of consciousness resulting from lack of oxygen or exposure to harmful substances including biological agents
- decompression sickness requiring immediate medical treatment (but excluding where this arises in work covered by the **Diving Operations at Work Regulations 1981**)
- any acute illness requiring medical treatment, plus any loss of consciousness resulting (in either case) from the absorption of any substance by inhalation, ingestion or through the skin
- acute illness requiring medical treatment where there is a reason to believe that this resulted from exposure to a pathogen or infected material
- any other injury which results in the injured person being admitted immediately into hospital for more than 24 hours or involves hypothermia, heat-induced illness or the need for resuscitation.

Accidents which result in absence from work for more than 3 days (including non-working days but excluding the day on which the accident occurred) must be reported on form

F2508 (revised) within 10 days of the accident. In the case of fatal accidents or major injury (see box on previous page), the enforcing authority must be notified immediately by the quickest practicable means (normally by telephone). A written report (on form F2508 (revised)) must also be made within 10 days of the accident.

Certain work-related diseases must also be reported under the regulations. Details of these are given on page 54.

It should be noted that the reporting rules on major injuries also apply to dangerous occurrences, ie potentially dangerous incidents such as the collapse of certain lifting equipment, accidental ignition of explosives or the release of large quantities of a highly flammable liquid, even if no injury is caused.

Records of reportable injuries must be kept for at least three years and must include the following details:

- date and time of the accident or dangerous occurrence
- full name and occupation of the person affected, including the nature of the injury or other condition
- place where the accident/dangerous occurrence happened
- brief description of the circumstances.

A photocopy of form F2508 (revised) as sent to the enforcing officer may be considered satisfactory compliance with this requirement.

Accidents Involving Non-employees

The regulations also relate to accidents involving non-employees where the accident involves the person being taken straight to hospital or where the accident occurred in connection with hospital work (excluding medical or dental treatment). The details required for records in such cases are similar to those for workplace accidents, except that instead of details of occupation, details of status (eg passenger, visitor) are required.

Civil Actions

In common law a duty of care is owed by one person to another. Failure to exercise that duty of care so that an injury results, may lead to the injured person suing the other in tort for damages.

Where health and safety at work is concerned, employers are bound both by common law and by statute (the **Health and Safety at Work, etc Act 1974**) to take reasonable care of the health, safety and welfare of their employees at work. It follows, therefore, that if a machine is not maintained properly and, as a result, an employee is injured, that employee will be able to sue the employer for damages in respect of the "pain, injury, loss and damage" suffered as a result of the accident. Such awards may be comparatively trivial if an employee has suffered pain but no financial loss or, at the other end of the scale, may be enormous if the injury was so severe that the employee had to give up work permanently.

It is therefore important for managers to bear in mind the possibility of a civil claim if an accident occurs. In particular nothing should be said to the victim which might imply that the company accepts liability for the accident. In more practical terms it is important that the manager ensures that statements are taken as soon as possible from people who witnessed the accident — before memories have faded and tales have been embellished. It is important that a full and accurate picture is obtained of why and how the accident occurred.

This information, which should preferably take the form of a detailed report, should also be sent to the company's insurers. It is, of course, essential that this report does not try to "whitewash" the company. If machinery or systems were faulty, remedial action must be taken immediately, or the machine taken out of service.

Criminal Action

If the accident resulted from a breach of law, eg the **Health and Safety at Work, etc Act 1974**, the organisation, or one of its officers, could face a criminal prosecution. The investigation required in the case of a civil claim would obviously be essential if the case were to be defended.

The offences and penalties under the Acts are set out in chapter 6 (see page 82).

Follow-up Procedures

The best time to review safety procedures is shortly after an accident has occurred. This is the one time when even the most blasé employees are likely to be receptive to the need for taking safety precautions. If the accident occurred because the employee had failed to wear safety equipment or, for example, had removed a guard in order to increase output, an explanation to other workers of the cause of the accident and its consequences will act as a powerful deterrent to others in taking similar short cuts.

The manager should also ensure that records are kept within the department of all accidents and "near misses". In this way trends which might indicate dangerous processes and systems or careless employees can be remedied before any serious injuries occur. Employees should be encouraged to report any potentially dangerous incidents and to offer suggestions as to how particular operations might be carried out more safely.

Whilst a nil accident record is a rarity in many workplaces, managers are uniquely placed to learn lessons from accidents and so to improve their departments' safety records.

First Aid

Rules for the provision of first aid facilities at work are laid down in the **Health and Safety (First Aid) Regulations 1981**.

The regulations place a general duty on employers to make, or ensure that there is made, adequate first aid provision for their employees. It is for the employer to assess what is adequate, bearing in mind factors such as: the distribution of employees; the nature of the work; the size and location of the establishment; shift working; distance from outside medical services and the number of employees.

First Aid Boxes

All employers must keep at least one first aid box. Sufficient quantities of each item should always be available in every first aid box or container. In most cases these will be as follows.

Checklist: First Aid Boxes

- a general guidance card
- 20 individually wrapped sterile adhesive dressings (assorted sizes) appropriate to the work establishment
- 2 sterile eye pads, with attachment
- 4 individually wrapped triangular bandages (preferably sterile)
- 6 safety pins
- 6 medium-sized individually wrapped sterile unmedicated wound dressings (approximately 12cm × 12cm)
- 2 large sterile individually wrapped unmedicated wound dressings (approximately 18cm × 18cm)
- 1 pair of disposable gloves.

Travelling first aid kits should be appropriate for the circumstances in which they are to be used. At least the following should be included:

- a general guidance card
- 6 individually wrapped sterile adhesive dressings
- 1 large sterile unmedicated dressing (approximately 18cm × 18cm)

- triangular bandages
- 2 safety pins
- individually wrapped moist cleansing wipes
- 1 pair of disposable gloves.

It is important to note that *only* the items listed above may be contained in first aid boxes — medicines such as aspirin or paracetamol should not be included.

First Aiders

The regulations specify that a "suitable person" is one that can render first aid to his or her employees at work. A "suitable person" is:

- a first aider who holds a current first aid certificate issued by an organisation approved by the HSE (where a workplace poses particular risk, a first aider will need additional training or specific training to be a "suitable person")
- any other person who has undergone training and obtained qualifications approved by the HSE.

Certain practising registered medical practitioners and practising nurses may also be regarded as first aiders.

In general the employer must provide, as a minimum, an "appointed" person at all times when a "suitable person" is temporarily or unavoidably absent while employees are at work. An "appointed person" is one who is to take charge of the situation, eg call an ambulance, if a serious injury or illness occurs during the absence of the first aider. Ideally the "appointed person" will be trained to administer emergency first aid if necessary.

The number of first aiders required for any particular workplace will depend on the nature of that workplace and the risks and hazards which it entails. It is for the employer to determine the adequacy of the provision of first aid facilities in the light of the circumstances pertaining to that particular workplace.

However, typically in low-risk situations, an employer will need at least one first aider during normal working hours for every 50 employees. In hazardous situations the employer should decide what number of first aiders will be adequate and appropriate, but this should not be less than one for every 50 employees.

Provision of Information

Employees must be notified of first aid arrangements and at least one notice should be conspicuously displayed giving the location of first aid equipment and facilities and the names and locations of first aid personnel.

Accident Book

In addition to the reporting requirements set out earlier in this chapter, a record of all injuries — however minor — must be kept in an accident book. Accident books are required at all premises which are covered by the **Factories Act 1961** or where 10 or more people are employed at any time. However, as a matter of best practice, it is recommended that an accident book should be kept even in premises where less than 10 people are employed. All premises should hold an easily accessible accident book and managers must explain to employees the need for it to be used appropriately. In addition, it must be retained for a period of three years from the date of the last entry. Employers can obtain an approved form of accident book from The Stationery Office.

3 Recognised Trade Unions

Where trade unions are recognised in the workplace, they have traditionally considered safety at work to be of major importance in their attempts to secure better working conditions for their members. Many managers will have come across this, even at the most superficial level, eg: "We need special equipment to do that job, it's unsafe otherwise!"; "My members can't be expected to work that long without a break — there could be an accident." Alternatively the representation may be linked with a more common plea, eg: "We should get extra pay for doing that job — it's dangerous/dirty/has unsocial hours, etc." Health and safety is thus often cited by shop stewards (in most cases, quite justifiably) as the reason for employees' concern over particular methods of working. In more formal settings full-time union officials are also quick to express their views where the health and safety of employees is concerned. In addition, the development of health and safety law has ensured that recognised unions have particular statutory rights to seek to promote safety in the workplace.

The Relevant Law

Regulations made under the **Health and Safety at Work, etc Act 1974** — the **Safety Representatives and Safety Committees Regulations 1977** (as amended) — gave recognised trade unions the right to appoint representatives from the employer's union workforce to carry out certain health and safety functions. The legislation allows safety representatives to investigate hazards, accidents and complaints by employees and to take up issues with managers or with the health and safety authorities. The regulations now require employers to consult "safety and employee representatives" on measures taken to implement the **Management of Health and Safety at Work Regulations 1992** (see page 8). This means that "representatives of employee safety" (employee representatives) must also be appointed in non-unionised workforces (see *Non-unionised Workforces*, page 31). The **Health and Safety at Work, etc Act 1974** itself requires employers to consult with such appointed safety representatives with a view to working together to promote health and safety in the workplace. The law thus creates important rights for all employees and obligations for employers.

Recognised Unions

Trade unions recognised by the employer have the legal right to appoint safety representatives with whom the employer must consult. A recognised union is a union with which the employer bargains over matters such as pay and conditions, termination of employment, disciplinary matters, etc. Unions have no automatic right to be recognised and it is entirely up to the organisation whether or not it is prepared to negotiate with the trade union concerned.

In order to take advantage of the safety representatives' rules the union must be recognised for collective bargaining purposes, not just for representation. In one case the union had been granted only the right to represent members in disciplinary or grievance proceedings. The courts ruled that this was not true recognition since it did not allow for bargaining or negotiations with the employer about terms and conditions of employment, etc.

Appointment of Safety Representatives

It may be surprising to learn that a recognised union has sole discretion as to whom it appoints as a safety representative. A manager who finds that the most unlikely person in the company has become an appointed representative can do nothing about it legally. Any failure to deal with the individual concerned in his or her official capacity could involve a breach of the legal obligation to consult with appointed safety representatives. There is only one main rule which governs the question of who can be appointed as a safety representative, namely that the person who is appointed should normally have had at least two years' service with the employer concerned or at least two years' experience in similar employment.

The appointment is made when the union notifies the employer in writing of the name of the safety representative and the group of employees that the individual will represent. There is no need for the person to be elected. The law states that once appointed the employee concerned will remain a safety representative until the union notifies the employer in writing that the appointment is ended, the representative resigns, or he or she ceases to be employed in the workplace.

The Representative's Rights

Managers must be aware what appointed safety representatives are entitled to do by law in order to deal effectively with the health and safety issues they may raise.

As the title implies, the representative's main right is to represent employees in consultations with the employer over health and safety issues. As the employer's representative, a manager's legal obligation is to consult with the safety and employee representatives to ensure that arrangements are made which enable both management and workforce to co-operate in promoting health and safety. In particular, as a result of the **Management of Health and Safety at Work Regulations 1992**, employers must consult safety and employee representatives on:

- the introduction of measures in the workplace substantially affecting the health and safety of employees
- arrangements for the appointment of "competent" persons (see page 8)

- the planning and organisation of health and safety training
- the provision of health and safety information, and
- the health and safety implications of new technology.

Managers must be prepared to discuss matters with safety and employee representatives, to listen to their point of view, and to give full consideration to their proposals. The approach should therefore be one of joint problem solving with both manager and representatives working together to promote safe practices.

Many unions see health and safety matters as well within the scope of collective bargaining and solutions acceptable to everyone can often be reached in this way. However, in terms of the absolute rights of safety representatives, managers are bound only to consult, not to bargain.

Main Functions

Apart from the right to represent employees in discussions with the employer, the law also requires safety representatives to carry out specific functions. These are:

- to investigate potential hazards and dangerous occurrences at the workplace and to examine the causes of accidents at the workplace
- to investigate complaints by the employees they represent relating to their health, safety and welfare
- to make representations to the employer on matters arising out of the two points above
- to make representations to the employer on general matters affecting the health, safety and welfare at work of the employees at the workplace
- to carry out inspections of the workplace
- to represent employees in consultation with inspectors from the Health and Safety Executive (HSE) and other enforcement authorities

- to receive information from inspectors on matters affecting employees' health, safety and welfare
- to attend meetings of safety committees (see below).

The law makes it clear that in carrying out these functions appointed safety representatives do not take on any extra legal responsibilities for their actions. If, for example, a representative proposes a particular course of action which is followed by management, but that results in a serious accident, the responsibility for the accident will virtually always fall on the employers. This means that, to some degree, safety representatives are in a privileged position, although as ordinary employees of the organisation they would still have general obligations under the **Health and Safety at Work, etc Act 1974** to take reasonable care for their own safety and that of others (see page 6).

Time Off Work

There is little point in the law providing for safety representatives to carry out particular functions unless they are also given a statutory amount of time in which to do this. The law therefore says that employers must allow appointed representatives to take such time off work, with pay, as is necessary for them to carry out their functions and to undergo such training in aspects of their role as is reasonable in all the circumstances. The words "necessary" and "reasonable" are the only guidelines that the law itself lays down and so assistance for managers in this area is somewhat limited.

To decide what is necessary, factors such as: the reason why the time off is requested; when it is needed; the amount of time required; and the number of people asking for time off at a given time, etc should all be considered. For example, suppose a serious accident has just occurred in the workplace; a request for immediate time off for representatives to investigate and satisfy themselves that there is no further danger to others is likely to be considered "necessary" by the law. On the other hand, immediate time off to record a standard report of a minor accident could legitimately be deferred if the employer's needs are more pressing. When it comes to training there are two issues concerned: is the training necessary in the first place and, if so, is it reasonable in the circumstances? When looking at whether training is necessary, the same type of considerations apply as for time off. In assessing whether the training is reasonable, the content of the training, its relevance to the workplace and whether or not the employer provides similar training might also be considered.

A code of practice approved by the HSE entitled *Safety Representatives and Safety Committees* provides some further guidance. It recommends that newly appointed representatives receive training approved by their union or the TUC soon after appointment and also that training is given where the representative has special responsibilities or relevant changes in the law occur. Incidentally, the code also recommends that when a safety representative's attendance on a course is requested by a union, the union should normally give advance notice and supply details of the course to the employer. Managers are therefore quite entitled to expect that this will be done.

When considering time off for safety matters it is up to the manager to adopt a flexible approach and to weigh up each request on its own merits when deciding whether representatives need time off in order to discharge their obligations. Ideally it is best to try and reach agreement with the union(s) in advance on the appropriate numbers and arrangements that will apply when time off is required.

Payment

Time off when granted should always be with pay, the general rule being that employees are paid what they would have received had they remained working for the period. When representatives are engaged on piecework, payment should be made on the basis of the average rate of pay (or a fair estimate of earnings made).

Enforcement

Inevitably, situations can arise where the employer disputes the necessity for time off and refuses to grant it. In this instance, or where the employer refuses to pay for time off given, the safety or employee representative can refer the case to an industrial tribunal for adjudication. When the tribunal upholds a complaint it can award such compensation as is just and equitable. The tribunal must award the pay due to the employee where the complaint is that time off has been allowed but no pay received.

Rights to Information

In addition to the rights outlined above, safety representatives are also entitled to inspect and take copies of any documents which the employer may be legally bound to keep under existing safety legislation (eg accident records) and which are relevant to the workplace or to the employees covered by the safety and/or employee representative. Individual health records are, however, specifically excluded.

Employers must also allow access to information necessary for safety and employee representatives to carry out their functions. The code of practice says that this might legitimately include:

- information about the employer's plans, performance and any changes proposed which may affect health and safety
- technical information on particular hazards — machinery, chemicals, processes, etc
- records and statistical information on accidents, notifiable diseases, etc
- results of any health and safety monitoring procedures which are carried out by management.

Certain information is excluded from these rules, for example information which is against the interests of national security and information which cannot be disclosed without breaking the law.

Safety representatives have to give reasonable notice in order to inspect documents. Again, managers should exercise discretion and adopt the same flexibility of approach applicable to requests for time off. Ideally the type of information which will be made readily available should be agreed in advance with unions.

Inspecting the Workplace

Appointed safety representatives have a statutory right to inspect workplace areas at least every three months, as long as they have given a reasonable amount of notice of their intention to do so. Inspections can be more frequent where, for example, the working conditions have changed or new information on particular hazards has been published (as long as the representative has consulted in advance with management).

Where a notifiable accident or dangerous occurrence takes place, a representative can also inspect the relevant areas of the workplace if, where reasonably practicable, the employer is notified in advance.

Where inspections are to be carried out, the employer must provide facilities which the representative may reasonably require, including facilities for independent investigation and private discussion with employees.

Inspections can be conducted by the representative alone or jointly with a member of management. The law entitles the employer to be present in the workplace during an inspection and it will often be appropriate, in any event, for a management representative to be available to observe proceedings and to give any advice which may be required. When expert knowledge is needed, the attendance of external specialists may also be appropriate. Ideally, this should be agreed in advance with the representative, along with the form that the inspection will take, eg a tour of the premises or a safety sample (ie focusing on one particular department, hazard, etc and inspecting for factors detrimental to health and safety).

Managers should never seek to obstruct safety representatives when an inspection is being conducted or be evasive when asked about processes, equipment, etc. Although disputes over what is and what is not dangerous or important will inevitably arise, with good sense on all sides a solution can usually be reached. It should be remembered that it is the employer's responsibility to ensure health and safety and it is therefore in everyone's best interests if the inspection identifies potential problems so that matters can be put right.

Following an inspection of the workplace, safety representatives may choose to make a report in writing to the employer, highlighting any processes, conditions, etc which they regard as unsafe. Both the code of practice and a guidance note on safety representatives and safety committees recommend that this is done. For this purpose a standard form (available from the HSE) can be used which contains space for the representative to detail particulars of any areas of concern and for both the representative and employer to sign. There is no reason why a manager should not be prepared to sign this particular form as long as the relevant details are correct. Signing the form itself does not imply that the employer agrees with, for instance, a safety representative's observations that certain processes are hazardous. It is really only a record of the fact that the representative has inspected the workplace and drawn management's attention to matters of concern. Of course where a safety representative identifies particular areas of concern, managers should immediately investigate further and satisfy themselves that steps are taken to eliminate the hazard or to provide a full explanation where remedial action is not taken. The guidance note recommends that such an explanation is given in writing to the representative. The appropriate section of the form referred to above would be adequate for this purpose.

Non-unionised Workforces

The **Health and Safety (Consultation with Employees) Regulations 1996** gave non-union members the right to be consulted on health and safety matters in very much the same way as members of trade unions. These regulations enacted the requirements of the Framework Directive that all employees must be consulted on health and safety matters. The regulations make provision for the appointment of "representatives of employee safety" (employee representatives) whose rights in relation to consultation are very similar to those of safety representatives appointed by trade unions (eg paid time off, access to information, etc).

Safety Committees

A safety committee can provide an effective means of ensuring that health and safety in the workplace is maintained and, in certain circumstances, the law allows appointed safety representatives to ask the employer to establish such a committee. This applies where two or more representatives request this in writing. The employer must first consult with them and other safety representatives in the workplace and then establish a committee within three months of the original request. A notice must be displayed showing who the members of the committee are.

HSE guidance recommends that the number of management representatives should not exceed the number of employee representatives. This is one of the points that can be agreed in consultation with appointed safety representatives. In deciding who should be a member, it is sensible to try to ensure that line management, supervisory and other staff are all represented. Usually appointed safety representatives themselves will be committee members, although this does not have to be the case. Other factors which will obviously have an influence are the size of the workforce, the processes involved, the nature of the premises, etc. It should also be considered whether or not ex officio members are to be appointed to the committee. For example, it may be necessary for technical expertise to be made available from time to time in the form of the company's chief engineer, chemist, etc.

The overall aim should be to ensure that enough people are involved to maximise the expertise and experience available and, most importantly, to ensure that the committee remains compact in size, concentrates on the issues concerned and does not degenerate into a talking shop which achieves nothing.

It is sensible to draw up the constitution of the committee, its terms of reference and any rules or procedures which will apply to it, eg who will chair it, whether decisions will be taken by majority vote or by the management in consultation with other committee members, etc. It must be remembered that the main purpose of a safety committee is to act as a safety watchdog, monitoring the systems through which the employer ensures health and safety at work. HSE guidance suggests that its responsibilities might, therefore, include studying accident records and statistics, considering safety reports prepared internally by management, by appointed safety representatives and by the enforcing authorities, and developing safety rules, procedures, training, etc.

Safety committees should not become a forum for "safety bargaining", where particular safety measures are traded off in exchange for concessions from employees. This is not the purpose of the exercise. The idea is that all those involved work together to find the best ways in which the employer can ensure that employees' health and safety at work is protected. This is not to say that there should not be compromise where disagreements occur. The more people involved, the more likely it is that different views will be expressed and a mutually acceptable solution need to be found. What is important is that solutions still remain appropriate and that formal bargaining is avoided.

Competent Persons

Under the **Management of Health and Safety at Work Regulations 1992**, all employers — whether or not they recognise a trade union — must appoint one or more "competent" persons to help them to comply with health and safety legislation. In some cases these may be employees. All such persons must be given adequate time and resources to carry out their function.

4 Company Safety Policy

Health and safety is one of the most important aspects of a manager's job. It should always be taken into account when considering how to control and plan work and how to manage the job through subordinate staff.

But how do managers find out exactly what the company expects of them with regard to health and safety standards? Many safety-conscious companies will have their concerns about health and safety built into staff training and will ensure that managers know exactly what their obligations are. In all cases, however, the clearest statement of what is expected of managers should be found in the company's health and safety policy.

Health and Safety Policy Statements

Employers who employ five or more people are required to have a health and safety policy statement. This is a written statement of general policy concerning the organisation of and arrangements for health and safety at work. Furthermore the statement should be regularly revised to take account of changing circumstances, including changes to technology, premises, etc.

The preparation of such a document is an important exercise in itself, since the act of writing a statement should clarify everyone's thoughts about the dangers and hazards that are associated with the particular business. It also provides an opportunity for employees to be made more aware of their obligations and to raise the level of safety consciousness throughout the organisation.

The company's health and safety policy must be brought to the attention of every employee. It should also be given to contractors or other people who work on the company's premises, either regularly or for long periods.

It is in this document that managers should discover the role they have to play in the safe operation of the organisation. Managers should ensure that they know where to find a copy of the company's health and safety policy, that they have read it and that they understand the part they play in its implementation.

Who Should Formulate the Policy?

The Health and Safety Executive (HSE) recommends that employers should think about their own policy statements in co-operation with the management team and other employees (and very often the trade union safety representatives) in order to ensure that the policy will be really effective. The use of consultants to draft a health and safety policy or the use of "off the peg" statements is not recommended because it is most important that the company's managers identify all their organisation's health and safety problems for themselves. The HSE has produced an outline document to help small businesses prepare their health and safety policy statements. This provides a useful framework to work with but the actual content of the statement must, of course, be provided by the employer and will be unique to each and every organisation.

Clearly the responsibility for the policy lies at the highest level of the company's operation. The people who have the authority should be providing the leadership to ensure that safety standards are kept high. Whoever is in charge of the preparation of a policy should be aware that they must produce a document which is both relevant and a valuable tool for managers and other employees in their place of work. For instance, simply quoting the asbestos regulations and then expecting ordinary people who are employed to strip asbestos out of buildings and to understand what is required of them is unacceptable. Only providing copies of the regulations which are obscure and difficult to read without offering further explanations is just as bad. The information must be pitched at the right level to be helpful.

Policy Content

Health and safety policy statements must include the following information:

- a general statement of policy concerning health and safety
- organisational arrangements for implementing the policy
- identification of specific hazards and a statement of the rules designed to deal with these.

Statement of Policy

The policy should be signed by the managing director or the most senior person in the company. This confirms the commitment of senior management, ie the board of directors, to fulfil the policy. The policy should be worded so that managers are in no doubt that, when faced with a genuine conflict between the demands of production and the demands of safety, they will be supported if they choose the latter.

The policy should also be dated to ensure that it is periodically reviewed in the light of new conditions.

The following statement (see page 38) is included only to give an example of a safety policy, and to illustrate the sort of detail which might be appropriate. Again, it has to be stressed that "off the peg" statements are ill-advised.

Employers operating in sectors of industry that are potentially more dangerous might have a considerably longer general policy statement, pinpointing the main hazards that should receive full attention.

Example: Health and Safety Policy

The board of directors wish to pursue a policy statement to promote health and safety at work and seek the co-operation of all employees for that purpose. The company will provide working conditions which comply with the relevant statutory requirements and officially approved codes of practice that are designed to ensure good standards of health and safety.

Particular regard will be paid to:

- providing information, instruction and supervision to enable all employees to contribute positively to their own health and safety at work
- electrical equipment and systems of work to ensure that they are safe and do not endanger health
- providing safe arrangements for the storage, handling and movement of materials and substances
- providing welfare facilities and benefits as far as is reasonably practicable, and
- providing safe means of access to and egress from places of work which are under the company's control.

Although the company operates in an industry that is of low risk, injuries and illnesses can happen in any environment and it is the board of directors' objective to reduce the incidence of these to an absolute minimum, not merely in keeping with, but surpassing, the best experience in other similar organisations.

Signed:
(Chief Executive)

Date:

Any campaigns or programmes aimed at improving health and safety, such as a campaign to ensure fewer accidents involving slipping, could also be highlighted in the general policy statement.

Organisational Arrangements for Implementing Policy

The second part of any health and safety policy must include:

- the allocation of responsibilities within the organisation, and
- the administrative procedures which put it into practice.

For managers this is the most important part of the policy statement because it should include the precise responsibilities of every tier of management in the organisation, eg directors, senior or departmental managers, managers, etc.

It should be possible to trace the exact line of responsibility leading from a junior employee to the individual with overall responsibility for health and safety in the organisation. Line managers should be able to see exactly where their responsibilities lie in relation to the company-wide safety policy.

Section Heads and Line Managers

Whilst senior management will usually have responsibility for establishing safety policies and procedures, managers are held directly responsible for their implementation. This responsibility is often limited to the safety of employees who report directly to them. However, equally important is a manager's responsibility for informing senior management (or the employer's safety officer) about any known or potential accident or any occupational health hazard associated with the operation under their control. In carrying out the organisation's safety policies and procedures, managers should ensure that:

- when planning each operation, safety considerations are an integral part of that planning
- all employees are properly instructed about the hazards of their jobs and how to avoid them
- where appropriate, the assistance of the company's safety specialist (or senior manager charged with such responsibilities) is sought on matters concerning safe practices and procedures
- essential safety equipment and devices are provided and used on each job performed under their supervision
- prompt corrective action is taken whenever unsafe conditions or unsafe actions by employees are noted
- all injuries are promptly treated and reported and that they themselves take a full part in investigations to find the causes of all accidents (even minor ones) so that corrective action can be taken to prevent a recurrence
- the safety status of the operation under their control is periodically checked, perhaps by using a safety checklist.

It is essential that line managers as well as senior managers promote a responsible attitude towards health and safety and provide leadership within their sphere of control to achieve this. If a manager does not care about what is going on neither will anyone else.

Managers may be responsible for the detailed administration of certain safety regulations, for instance ensuring that grindstones are replaced by appropriately trained people. In other environments a manager's responsibilities will be more concerned with ensuring through managing staff that people work in a safe and healthy manner. In many cases management is the key to promoting a safety conscious attitude.

Putting the Policy into Practice

No policy would be complete without details of procedures that affect health and safety, ie first aid arrangements, fire arrangements, reporting accidents or dangerous occurrences, procedure for raising a health and safety grievance, etc. All managers need to be familiar with such procedures since they will probably be called upon to use them from time to time.

Example: First Aid Procedure
"The company provides first aid boxes in every department of the factory; more extensive first aid treatment can be obtained from the nurse in the medical room. Employees are encouraged to make full and proper use of these facilities. In some circumstances the company will provide a small travelling first aid kit for employees whose work frequently takes them away from their base. The list of employees trained to undertake first aid is posted on the company notice-board. Any employee wishing to undertake first aid training by an approved organisation such as the British Red Cross Society can apply for assistance to undertake training."

Example: Accident Procedure
"All accidents involving injury, however trivial, should be notified to the immediate superior by or on behalf of the individual concerned. Details of the accident will be entered in the accident book, which is kept in the medical room. Staff should also report any dangerous occurrences which take place even where these have not resulted in injury. This is to ensure that remedial action is taken to prevent such dangerous occurrences happening again."

Emergency Procedure

Special consideration should be given to precautionary procedures for dealing with any special hazards relating to the premises, processes or work activity. This is particularly relevant when flammable, explosive, toxic, corrosive, or any other substance likely to be harmful to employees, is being handled. It is also worth checking whether the work carried out in premises next door or opposite could give rise to an emergency situation to which employees will have to respond quickly, eg risk of leaking chemicals, risk of explosion, etc.

Safety Grievance Procedure

The handling of health and safety grievances can often be effectively channelled through a grievance procedure designed specifically to handle complaints or deal with disputes over health and safety problems. It is not unusual for such complaints to develop into disciplinary problems, eg where an employee stubbornly or unreasonably refuses to work on a particular machine or process which is demonstrably safe to use. The procedure should, therefore, allow for disciplinary action to be taken as well as remedial action to deal with the health and safety problem.

Grievance procedures should include the name and job title of the person to contact if employees are dissatisfied with the result of their first complaint. Employees should also know who to contact in the event of a real risk of death or serious injury or a severe health risk which requires urgent action. These people should have the necessary authority to take effective steps. The procedure should ensure that complaints are investigated with urgency.

Safety Rules and Practice

Health and safety policy statements should also cover the detailed operational requirements that will ensure a healthy and safe working environment. Very often these are in the form of company safety rules or a code of safe practice.

Managers can make a valuable contribution to the drafting and implementation of this part of the policy because of their detailed knowledge of the work area.

When drafting company safety codes it is always sensible to state the obvious even though it may seem very trivial and a matter of common sense. The following examples show what might be included in specific circumstances.

Example: Work Area that is Predominantly Clerical

Notice to Employees

- Bear in mind that undue haste and forgetfulness cause many, if not most, office accidents.
- Do not run down steps. Please use handrails going up or down stairs.
- Do not leave lower filing drawers open because this can cause trips and falls.
- Wipe up spilled drinks, wet patches or other fluid immediately to prevent accidents.
- Do not allow electrical and telephone cords to lie uncovered on the floor since they are major tripping hazards.
- Keep floor areas free of obstructions; waste-baskets, briefcases and other objects should not be left in aisles. Office furniture should be arranged to ensure that it does not project into aisles.
- Pointed objects such as pencils, pens, letter openers, files, etc must be used carefully to avoid puncture wounds.

Example: Work on Building Sites

Notice to Employees

- Watch out for warning notices on site and equipment and obey the warnings given.
- Avoid interfering with ladders, altering scaffolding or moving boards unless authorised to do so.
- Wear protective clothing or equipment when provided and wear it as instructed.
- Check equipment for any damage before and after use and report any damage at the earliest opportunity.
- Clean, maintain and carry equipment safely.
- Obtain help if a load is awkward or heavy; objects should not obstruct vision when being carried.

Machinery

It is a good idea to take a close look at items of machinery and to set out rules regarding their use. It is not sufficient merely to refer to the relevant codes of practice or operating instructions; managers should also highlight the rules for safe operation and incorporate local safety procedures as shown below.

Example: Operating Guillotines

The operator must check that the rear guard is in position and is secure before switching on power to start the guillotine.

After a cutting operation the power is to be switched off at the mains wall switch before lifting the guard to remove cut material; after removal the guard is to be replaced securely.

Scrap ends are to be removed at least once a day and the power is to be switched off each evening.

Example: Operating Bandsaws

The operator must ensure that all guards are secure before switching on the mains wall switch.

During any cleaning, adjustments or alterations to settings, the mains power is to be switched off at the wall switch.

Each evening the machine is to be left clean and tidy, with the power switched off. Swarf is to be placed in the special trolley provided.

At the end of the working week the machine is to be stripped down, cleaned thoroughly, oiled and greased where required, and reassembled.

The area around the bandsaw is to be kept clean and tidy.

Other Areas

The above points are only a general indication of the sort of areas which will need attention. Each workplace poses its own special risks and hazards. Managers are uniquely placed to alert those responsible for drawing up the safety policy to factors which should be given special mention.

5 Recognising Employees' Health Problems

Why should employers take an interest in the health of their employees? There are a number of very good reasons. Employers will be anxious to keep sickness absence to an absolute minimum and, when their staff are at work, they will want to be sure that they are fit and well so that they can give their best. There is also the fact that the law requires employers to do all that can reasonably be expected to safeguard the health of those who work for them. They may face prosecution under the **Health and Safety at Work, etc Act 1974** if they fail in that duty. However, many employers simply feel that they have a moral duty to take an interest in the well-being of their staff and often go beyond what is actually required by law.

There are a number of ways employers try to ensure that they have a fit and healthy workforce. These include screening employees when they join the organisation and at regular intervals during employment, providing private medical insurance either free of charge or at specially reduced rates and setting up some sort of in-house health service which employees can use.

All of these things can be extremely useful in helping employers meet their various duties and obligations, but they are by no means the end of the story. Medically trained staff will at best see employees only from time to time, whereas managers are with them every working day. This daily contact is ideal for spotting potential health problems (and health risks within the workplace) at an early stage so that appropriate action can be taken. It is the manager who is likely to be the first to spot that a fork-lift truck driver is developing a drink problem which might lead to an accident on the factory floor. It is the manager who might be first to notice that the machine operator who has been with the company for 40 years is not as nimble as he used to be and is starting to make mistakes. It is the manager who hears all the daily moans and groans about aches and pains, problems and worries.

The job of ensuring that the workforce remains fit and well, therefore, cannot just be left to the company doctor or the health and safety officer. It is a responsibility which must be shared by everyone and not least by managers. Much can be achieved by simply keeping eyes and ears open for possible problems. Signs might include a deterioration in job performance or output, changes in personality or attitude, increased levels of lateness or absenteeism, and physical changes such as weight loss or gain or a decline in general appearance.

Where a manager thinks that an employee has a health problem of some sort, he or she will need to judge how best to deal with it. It may be a question of taking the individual aside, talking the problem over and perhaps suggesting that the matter be referred to the personnel officer or company doctor. It may involve urging the person to visit his or her GP if this seems more appropriate or if there is a reluctance to see anyone connected with work.

In other cases it may be necessary for the manager to alert a senior colleague or the personnel department to the problem without the employee's consent or knowledge. Much will depend on the nature of the problem and who is involved and managers will need to use their skill and experience when deciding how to handle individual situations. Advice on how to recognise and deal with some of the health problems which commonly occur within the workplace is given later in this chapter.

Recruiting People with Health Problems

Some of the health problems that managers have to deal with are known about from the time an employee is taken on. When people are recruited they may reveal certain facts about their state of health either at interview or when they fill in application forms or medical questionnaires. Sometimes a pre-employment medical examination may bring to light a health problem which the individual has not mentioned or perhaps not even known about.

Pre-employment Screening

In some industries employees must have a medical examination by law before they can start work. This includes, for example, those working in diving operations and those whose work involves dealing with ionising radiations. In some cases check-ups are also required at regular intervals throughout the period of employment.

Apart from situations where pre-employment screening is required by law, screening also makes sense where a high standard of mental or physical fitness is needed to do a job properly, and where jobholders or their colleagues could be put at risk if these standards were not met. Pre-employment screening is often also required where securing a job carries with it membership of a pension or life assurance scheme.

When someone applies for a job and a particular health problem is revealed, the employer will usually look to a medical advisor for help in deciding whether or not the person should be recruited. Managers may also be asked for their opinion at this stage as to whether or not it would be feasible for a particular job to be done by the person concerned. For example, it might be felt that a disabled person could be taken on if certain reasonable adjustments were made to the work process or the environment and the manager might be asked to consider how this could be achieved. In another situation it might be felt that the best candidate for the job is someone who needs regular time off for medical treatment, such as renal dialysis, and the manager might be asked to consider whether working hours could be made more flexible to accommodate this problem.

At all times managers must bear in mind that people who have a long-term disability are protected by the provisions of the **Disability Discrimination Act 1995** (see *Croner's Reference Book for Employers*). The legislation requires employers to make reasonable adjustments in the workplace to allow for a pre-existing or developing condition to be accommodated where an employee or potential employee is otherwise able to carry out the work.

Once employees with particular health problems have been appointed, the manager will have an important role in managing the situation. This may include helping the employees concerned to settle in, working with them to overcome any difficulties that arise, assessing how they cope with the job, reporting progress back to senior management and liaising with the personnel department and medical staff as necessary. The manager's role in all these matters will vary according to the nature of the employees' problems. For instance, an individual may suffer from a condition that cannot be cured but which is controlled in some way, such as asthma. The manager's role in such cases will be to keep the problem in mind and to know how to recognise and deal with it should an employee get into difficulties. In other instances the manager may be asked to keep an eye on a particular employee with a view to reporting back if any problems develop. Examples might include someone taken on with a history of mental illness or alcoholism. Sometimes the manager may be asked to keep certain health problems in mind when work is being organised and allocated. For example, someone with a back problem will need to avoid heavy lifting; another with dermatitis might need to avoid contact with certain substances.

Where managers are entrusted with privileged information about an employee's state of health, complete confidentiality must be maintained. Unfortunately this sometimes puts managers in an awkward position. They might feel that making other members of staff aware of an individual's health problem will actually benefit the person concerned. One example would be certain cases of epilepsy where work colleagues might need to know how to recognise and cope with fits. Where managers are unsure about what and how much to disclose to others, they should discuss the matter with the individual involved and also seek advice from a senior colleague or the personnel department.

Health Problems which Develop During Employment

Of course many health problems do not exist or are not known about when an employee is taken on; they develop at a later stage. Once again the manager's role in dealing with these will vary according to the nature of the problem. To start with, there are all the usual short-term illnesses from which most people suffer at one time or another. Colds, flu, throat or chest infections, stomach bugs, etc — the list is endless. After a few days or weeks away from work the employee will resume normal working. Managers know only too well what to do in these situations. It is usually a question of receiving and dealing with notification in one form or another, organising cover for the person's absence and possibly even arranging a "get well soon" card. Of course some problems do crop up with short-term illness and the manager's duties in dealing with these can be as diverse as persuading the over-conscientious employee with a bad cold to go home before infecting everyone else, or issuing a warning to the employee who constantly takes sick leave on Mondays to get over the weekend's hangover.

At the other end of the scale there are the more serious health problems which may make it difficult or even impossible for employees to continue in their existing jobs. Illnesses may develop very rapidly and a person may go from being perfectly healthy to being on long-term absence within a short period. Here the manager's role will probably be limited to reallocating workloads or organising temporary cover until the person returns or a replacement is found. In other cases, however, a serious health problem will develop far more gradually — perhaps over a period of months or years — and the manager will be very much involved in monitoring and managing the work situation in conjunction with personnel and medical staff. Examples would include arthritis, heart disorders, deteriorating eyesight or hearing, back problems, alcoholism and mental illness, as well as certain specifically work-related diseases such as occupational dermatitis and occupational respiratory disorders.

Health Surveillance

In some situations, employers are required by law to ensure that their employees' health is properly monitored. For example, under the **Management of Health and Safety at Work Regulations 1992**, where a risk assessment has revealed that a work activity may cause a particular disease or problem, then health surveillance will be appropriate. The **Control of Substances Hazardous to Health Regulations 1994** state that health surveillance is necessary where employees are engaged in certain work processes or are exposed to certain substances. Even where substances are not specifically listed, employers must assess whether they might be harmful and whether health checks are appropriate. Regular medical examinations are also required by law in certain occupations, eg HGV drivers and aircraft pilots.

In other areas, employers simply provide health screening as a way of helping to fulfil their health and safety responsibilities or as part of a welfare service. They may consist of general health check-ups or more specialised attention such as screening for breast or cervical cancer.

Although these procedures can be absolutely crucial in detecting problems at an early stage, they do not lessen the need for managers to be alert to the early signs and symptoms of disease. Noticing the occurrence and frequency of problems such as coughing, headaches, breathlessness, dizziness, tiredness, aches and pains, and knowing when to refer a matter on for further investigation all form an important part of the manager's role in safeguarding employees' health and welfare.

Work-related Diseases

Some health problems arise not just during employment but wholly or partly because of it. Naturally employers have a special responsibility to their employees in this area. In some cases the connection between ill-health and work has been clearly established. One notorious example is the link between respiratory problems and mine working. However, there are also less obvious examples such as the much debated possible side-effects of using VDUs (see page 105). The wide range of problems that can arise relates very much to the nature of the work being undertaken and employers have a responsibility to be aware of, and to guard against, those which are linked to their particular area of work.

Work-related health problems may be caused by any of the following.

Checklist: Health Risks at Work

- Physical aspects of the job, eg noise-induced deafness; joints damaged by repeated vibration or friction (such as beat hand); back injuries from constant bending or lifting.
- Exposure to certain substances used in the workplace, eg skin cancer from tar, pitch or bitumen or poisoning by lead, mercury or arsenic.
- Biological agents, eg viral hepatitis or AIDS from contact with human blood products.
- Miscellaneous factors, eg pneumoconiosis, asbestosis and lung cancer from exposure to various sorts of dust.
- Stress linked to a variety of workplace causes, eg excessive hours, poor job design, etc.

Managers have a vital role to play in preventing and recognising work-related diseases. This will involve their being alert to any signs which might indicate that a health problem or health risk exists or is developing. Because managers work closely with employees on a daily basis they are the ones who are best placed for detecting and reporting such problems at an early stage. Another aspect of the manager's role in this area is to ensure that any measures which have been introduced to protect the health of employees are being observed in full. This may include making sure that proper use is made of special washing and eating facilities, extractor fans, splash guards and cleaning equipment. It will also include ensuring that employees maintain a second line of defence against health hazards by using any personal protection that is provided in the form of overalls, aprons, sleeves, gloves, masks, goggles, earmuffs, breathing apparatus, barrier creams and so on. However, even when managers have satisfied themselves that all health and safety rules and procedures are being observed, they cannot afford to sit back and relax. Part of their role is also to be on the look out for ways in which existing measures could be improved and to help identify sources of danger which up to now have gone undetected.

Reportable Diseases

Although much has been done to reduce work-related illnesses, they have by no means been eradicated and remain a cause for great concern. So that the Government can keep track of those problems which still exist, and take appropriate action, employers are required under the **Reporting of Injuries, Diseases and Dangerous Occurrences Regulations 1995** to report cases of specified occupational diseases as they arise. Where employees suffer from one of the diseases listed in the regulations and their work falls into one of the categories specified, a report must be sent to the enforcing authority (usually the Health and Safety Executive (HSE) or the relevant local authority) on form F2508A. In some cases this task may fall to the manager. A report need only be made once a written diagnosis has been received from a doctor on, for example, a medical certificate. As well as notifying the enforcing authority, the regulations also require that a record is kept of the details for at least three years. Probably the easiest way of doing this is to take and retain a photocopy of the completed form F2508A. The full list of diseases and occupations forms part of the relevant regulations and is also available from HSE area offices. It includes the following.

Checklist: Reportable Health Problems

- Poisoning by certain substances, eg arsenic, mercury or phosphorous.
- Certain skin diseases, eg ulceration, inflammation or cancer of the skin.
- Certain respiratory diseases, eg occupational asthma or lung cancer.
- Certain infections, eg hepatitis, TB or illness caused by a dangerous pathogen.
- Other conditions, eg bone cancer, cataracts and white finger.

As stated above, a report is made only where the employee is both suffering from one of the listed diseases *and* engaged in the type of work specified.

Occupational Dermatitis

This is the most common occupational disease. Dermatitis is a skin inflammation caused by contact with one or more substances and, when the condition arises from substances used at work, it is called occupational dermatitis. It is usually the individual's hands, wrists or arms that are affected. The problem usually starts with redness, soreness and irritation, followed by the formation of blisters which may crack open and form crusts. The condition is certainly miserable for the person concerned and may be unsightly but it is not normally infectious.

Dermatitis may be caused by *irritants* or *sensitisers*. Irritants irritate and damage the skin directly and may be either chemical, eg certain acids and alkalis, or physical, eg heat or friction. They can cause a reaction when the skin is exposed to them and the more contact there is, the worse the condition gets. Sensitisers can cause an allergic response in the skin. Almost anything can cause a skin allergy, but common sensitisers include certain woods, plastics, dyes, adhesives and insecticides. Their effect is rather less straightforward than that of irritants because initial contact with the substance may lead to an allergic response which is not actually visible. It will become obvious only when there is further contact and the familiar skin reaction develops.

The onset of dermatitis may occur as soon as an individual is exposed to a substance or may happen after many years of contact. There are no hard and fast rules. As for preventing occupational dermatitis, the manager's role includes being aware of the hazardous properties of substances used in his or her workplace, encouraging good skin hygiene (eg frequent wiping and washing) and ensuring that protective clothing and barrier creams are used where necessary. In dealing with actual cases, the manager will need to keep an eye open for early signs of the problem so that affected individuals can be encouraged to seek medical advice and appropriate protective measures can be taken. In some cases people suffering from dermatitis may need to be transferred to work where contact with the offending substance can be avoided. Unhappily where this is not possible and the condition worsens, dismissal on ill-health grounds may be the end result for the person concerned. This, however, may lead to a claim for industrial injury and this must be avoided if at all possible by dealing with the issue as soon as it occurs.

Dust-related Health Problems

Dust in the workplace can adversely affect the skin (eg dermatitis) and the eyes (eg conjunctivitis), but potentially the biggest health problem it can cause is respiratory disease. The dust may be from vegetable products such as wood, cork and grain or from inorganic substances such as asbestos and cement. Exposure to vegetable dust may cause either direct irritation of the respiratory passages resulting in coughs, tightness of the chest and, eventually, lung disease, or it may lead to an allergic response in the form of asthma.

In a similar way, inorganic dusts can cause either direct irritation or an allergic reaction, but they can also cause harm through being either poisonous (eg metal compounds such as lead) or by causing tissue changes in the respiratory system. This is what happens in the well-known dust-related diseases such as asbestosis and silicosis. Certain dusts may also considerably increase the risk of contracting lung cancer.

The manager's role in dealing with dust-related health problems is most importantly that of prevention. Whilst some of the conditions listed above show themselves at an early stage, many may not come to light for a considerable number of years. Where people do not feel that their health is being damaged, they can become blasé about protection and prevention. This is particularly true in relation to dust. The prime responsibility of the employer is to eradicate or minimise the prevalence of dusts in the workplace. If the nature of the work precludes this, the appropriate protective measures must be taken. Where this includes the use of personal protective equipment (PPE) then it is the employee's duty to use it. It is the employer's duty to ensure that employees are properly trained in the use of such equipment and to ensure that employees do actually make use of it.

Prevention is of paramount importance because by the time many respiratory problems come to light the damage will already have been done. Having said that, early detection can lead to effective remedial action being taken in some cases, and so the manager needs to be alert to problems such as breathlessness, coughing and chest pain, and to ensure that these are investigated swiftly.

Occupational Asthma

Individuals can become sensitised to certain dusts (eg cereal dusts) and can develop asthma. But this sensitisation process is not confined to dust. Occupational asthma can result from exposure to a whole range of materials used at work. The manager should be on the look out for any employee who develops a wheeze or persistent dry cough when exposed to certain materials. The problem may even come to light by individuals mentioning that these symptoms develop when they go home. Such problems must be reported because occupational asthma requires skilled medical investigation to identify which substance or substances are responsible so that appropriate measures can be taken. Asthma arising from some agents is classified as a "prescribed" disease and is therefore reportable to the HSE (see *Reportable Diseases* on page 54).

Managers should obviously bear in mind the fact that some individuals suffer from asthma quite apart from their work situation. Pre-employment screening should ensure that if there is any possible additional risk to asthmatics it is discussed before they start employment.

Work-related Upper Limb Disorders

Over the last decade, one particular group of employment-related medical conditions has received an increasing amount of attention. This group consists of a variety of musculoskeletal problems, particularly relating to the upper limbs, which appear to be caused, or made worse by, certain occupations. Until recently, the term repetitive strain injury (RSI) was widely used to describe problems of this sort. However, since it has never been clear just which conditions fall under this heading, and since it is now recognised that repetition is just one factor amongst many, the term RSI has lost favour. The preferred expression is now "work-related upper limb disorders", which is used to describe a whole range of musculoskeletal problems which can affect the hand, wrist, arm or shoulder.

Typically upper limb disorders (ULDs) are found amongst those engaged in repetitive keyboard or assembly work. Signs that an employee may be developing a ULD problem should be taken seriously. It is all too easy to dismiss complaints of aching wrists or tingling fingers as an unavoidable "occupational hazard". However, in some cases, such problems can escalate into a permanent and disabling condition. During recent years, a number of claims have been made against employers for damage suffered, and large amounts of compensation have been paid out as a result. Such is the controversy surrounding the condition, however, that there has been a very mixed response to those bringing claims. One High Court judge provoked a storm of protest by describing RSI as "meaningless" when a case was brought before him. In contrast — just a few months later — a former typist was awarded a record £79,000 in an out-of-court settlement for the same condition.

Obviously some jobs are such that a certain amount of repetitive movement is inevitable, and it could be argued that little can be done to change this. However, in many cases, the way in which the person is sitting or standing, or the positioning of equipment or furniture, or the way in which a task is carried out, may contribute significantly to the problem. Changes in working practices may make all the difference with, for example, shorter but more regular rest periods. It may be possible to rotate workloads so that no employee is carrying out one particular movement continuously. Equipment may need to be adjusted or modified to fit individual requirements. Managers can be very much involved in spotting potential or existing problems and suggesting solutions. Genuine complaints about work-related pain or discomfort should, of course, be referred to management without delay. If a ULD is diagnosed early on, it may be possible to prevent further damage. If it goes undetected, permanent damage may result. As with all health and safety matters, when it comes to dealing with ULDs the golden rule is that prevention is better than cure.

General Health Problems

Smokers and Ill-health

Smokers may become ill with problems ranging from a tendency for them to develop chest problems when they have a cold, to the risk of their developing far more serious conditions, including lung cancer. Of course, where such problems do arise they will need to be tackled through the normal ill-health procedures for either frequent absence or long-term sickness. However, employers may also wish to become actively involved in helping smokers in their workforce to give up the habit. This may either be part of a strategy to help employees reduce their sickness absence or part of an attempt to create a smoke-free workplace. It may involve allowing time off for therapy or attendance on courses or, in larger companies, may extend to running courses in-house. It needs to be recognised that when heavy smokers are in the process of giving up, unpleasant physical effects are common such as headaches, sweating, shaking and of course craving. As a result, even people who are normally quite cheerful and sociable may become depressed, irritable or aggressive, and may find that their powers of concentration and levels of performance deteriorate rapidly. The manager can play an important role both in giving support and encouragement to would-be non-smokers, and in smoothing things over with colleagues who may be suffering as a result of jangling nerves and short tempers.

Both parties may need reassurance that the problems are only temporary and that with patience and understanding they can be overcome.

Passive Smoking

The biggest problem area associated with smoking in the workplace and ill-health is that of "passive smoking" (ie inhaling smoke from other people's cigarettes). The subject of passive smoking is receiving an increasing amount of attention and publicity and evidence is mounting to suggest that subjecting non-smokers to smoke may be putting their health at considerable risk. As the link between passive smoking and damage to health becomes more firmly established, more and more employers are acknowledging that they have a duty to protect their non-smoking employees from the hazards of tobacco smoke under the provisions of the **Health and Safety at Work, etc Act 1974**. Indeed, there have been claims that a refusal to introduce a smoking ban constitutes a breach of an employer's duty under that Act. It is not surprising, therefore, that many employers are already taking action by introducing designated smoking and no-smoking areas or smoking bans. Bans can cause much upset among smokers, especially as they are likely to suffer from the withdrawal symptoms outlined above if they cannot smoke at all during their hours at work. In some extreme cases heavy smokers might even be forced to resign from an organisation which introduces a total smoking ban.

If possible, therefore, less drastic measures such as restricting smoking to break periods and setting aside a smokers' rest room would appear to be a good compromise. However, provided a no-smoking rule is introduced sensibly with advance warning of when it is to start and the penalties that will be imposed for non-compliance, persistent offenders may be dismissed fairly.

If employers wish to avoid altogether the health problems associated with smoking, they *can* recruit only non-smokers into the workforce. Such discrimination is not unlawful. However, a policy of this sort might mean that some otherwise extremely good candidates are lost, and a balanced smoking policy within the organisation might well be preferable.

Stress

A subject which is receiving more and more attention amongst employers these days is how to deal with the adverse effects of stress. Their jobs may or may not be the source of worry for stressed employees, but either way their work is very likely to be affected. Both job performance and relationships with other employees may suffer and absenteeism may increase significantly. Indeed, it is thought that mental ill-health now accounts for a substantial proportion of lost working days each year. It is worth remembering that an employer's duty to protect employees from health and safety risks at work applies to both physical and mental illness. In one recent case, a former employee successfully claimed compensation for a nervous breakdown which he said was the direct result of stress at work.

There are many potential sources of stress at work and the variety of these serves to demonstrate what an individual matter stress is. For most people a certain amount of stress is actually helpful, and many would acknowledge the fact that they can only give their best when they are under some pressure.

However, beyond a certain point the undesirable effects of stress start to become apparent. The nature and level of this threshold varies considerably from person to person. For example, a repetitious job on an assembly line with no promotion prospects will suit one person perfectly whilst frustrating and depressing another. Equally a dynamic and responsible executive post will motivate and satisfy one person whilst causing another to feel inadequate and unable to cope.

Outside work, potential sources of stress are just as varied, although certain life experiences such as moving house, divorce, the birth of a child or bereavement are recognised generally as common causes of stress.

Problems may build up over a period, with individuals feeling increasingly stressed as their home and/or work situations develop. Alternatively, they may suddenly erupt in the wake of a particular event.

Just as the sources of stress vary from person to person, so do the ways in which the problem manifests itself. In many cases there is a change in behaviour or personality which may include the individual becoming impatient, irritable or bad tempered and finding it difficult to get on with other people. As far as work is concerned, performance is likely to deteriorate and, in some cases, this may be in spite of the fact that the individual is trying harder and working longer hours than ever before. Other signs worth looking out for include changed patterns in eating, drinking or smoking, self-neglect and obsessional behaviour. There may be a marked increase in absenteeism but, as already mentioned, working long hours and a reluctance to take time off can also be danger signs.

Managers are ideally placed for spotting signs of stress amongst their subordinates at an early stage and offering help either directly or by referring the problem to the personnel or occupational health function. Working closely with their staff should enable managers to get to know the individual personalities and be familiar with the sorts of circumstances that are likely to result in stress. This will make it easier for them to detect and even anticipate problems before they become serious.

As well as knowing and observing the people involved, it is worth being vigilant; the signs of stress outlined above may well result in complaints from other staff, whether these are received directly or are overheard in the corridor or canteen. Relationships between affected employees and their colleagues may well become strained and, if the problem is not dealt with promptly, may result in a sufferer becoming an outcast. Once relationships have broken down in this way, harmony can be difficult to restore, so the manager should intervene at an early stage to encourage sympathy and understanding amongst those involved.

There are also some individuals who suffer throughout their lives from some form of mental illness. When such cases are known to exist, a watchful eye should be kept on those concerned to ensure that the working environment does not exacerbate the condition and for any remedial action to be taken.

Unhappily, stress may result in the affected employee becoming incapable of performing adequately and in such circumstances the organisation's ill-health procedures will need to be followed. This may lead to long periods of sickness absence or even dismissal. It is hoped, however, that such cases can be kept to a minimum by the careful matching of people to jobs and by offering help and support to those experiencing difficulties.

Ageing

An issue which may cause problems at work, but which is often neglected, is the deterioration in health that can occur as people get older. Specific ailments can develop or worsen with age and these will need to be dealt with as described elsewhere. However, the less obvious effects of ageing may also need to be faced. As people get older, they may become less physically and mentally able. No hard and fast rules apply in this area, so managers need to watch out for any problems which might develop. For example, those employed in jobs requiring physical effort may find their work increasingly difficult to cope with as they get older. As time goes on, they may be putting themselves and others at risk. Deterioration in hearing and eyesight commonly form part of the ageing process. A transfer to lighter duties or even early retirement may be appropriate and the manager has an important part to play in judging when to recommend this. The task is often made more difficult by employees' reluctance to admit that they can no longer do as much as they could, and they may even do all in their power to conceal their difficulties. Problems may even come to light via comments or complaints from subordinates or colleagues.

In some cases the problem may be one of mental deterioration and memory can be one of the first things to suffer. Again, a sideways move or easing the person out of the organisation may be the answer.

In dealing with problems of ageing, employers need to balance their desire to be kind and sympathetic against the need to meet their business requirements and to fulfil their responsibilities under the **Health and Safety at Work, etc Act 1974**. Many people find growing older difficult to accept and tactless handling of related problems can leave employees feeling bitter about the organisation to which they have devoted many years of loyal service. An unhappy end to a working life can mar the years of retirement as well as the memories of what went before, and will benefit neither the individual nor the organisation's reputation.

In handling problems of ageing, managers may be tempted to leave well enough alone until matters come to a head, but this is not really the best course of action. By that time the employee may well have lost the respect of colleagues and have caused considerable damage to the business. Although it may not always be possible, helping employees face up to the problem firmly but gradually through counselling, with a view to agreeing a mutually acceptable course of action, is likely to be a better option for all concerned.

From a positive perspective, however, it must be remembered that older workers have the benefit of experience and maturity which offset the ageing process. The majority of people are perfectly capable of working to retirement age and beyond without any deterioration in performance.

Drug Abuse

There is no particular type of person who is prone to drug abuse. Employers should bear this in mind and be careful that they do not concentrate all their attention on young employees, only to miss addiction among more senior and established ranks. Experience shows that it is wise to keep an open mind about who might be vulnerable to drug abuse.

Where a drug problem is discovered in the workplace, the employer's concern will centre on a number of issues:

- the obvious damage being caused to the relevant employee's health
- the potential damage to other employees, both in terms of an increased risk of accidents and the possibility that they may be tempted to experiment with drugs
- the potential damage to the business resulting from increased absence levels and poor performance
- the fact that, except in certain specific circumstances, anyone keeping, taking or supplying controlled drugs or knowingly allowing this to happen on their premises will be guilty of a criminal offence.

In the light of all these factors, employers might be forgiven for thinking that they are bound to be on safe ground if they dismiss an employee for involvement in drug abuse. However, automatic dismissal in such circumstances will not necessarily be fair or appropriate. For example, when faced with an employee who has committed a drug offence *outside* work, the employer will need to decide whether this has any relevance to the actual employment situation. Even when drug abuse has occurred at work, it may be more appropriate to treat the problem initially as one of ill-health rather than misconduct, with the offer of help and time off for treatment.

Managers are ideally placed for spotting the early signs of drug abuse amongst employees. Although these will vary according to the drug being used, commonly they include extreme over-activity (hyperactivity), weight loss, fatigue (resulting from an inability to sleep), sudden changes in mood or behaviour and a deterioration in performance, attendance or timekeeping. These symptoms, however, could also be indicative of stress or a wide range of ill-health issues, so care should be taken before jumping to conclusions.

If an employee is actually under the influence of drugs at work, it is worth bearing in mind that he or she may simply appear to be drunk; signs of intoxication of any sort need careful investigation.

Where drug abuse is concerned, the substances that readily come to mind are cannabis, heroin, cocaine, ecstasy and LSD. Any evidence of these drugs, or the equipment used for administering them, will require swift action on the part of the manager. However, as most people now realise, many everyday substances can also be misused. The list includes glues, solvents, cleaning fluids and polishes, many of which may be essential in the workplace for a variety of purposes. Managers will do well to familiarise themselves with the different substances being used or stored in their particular workplace, and to identify those which could be misused and the symptoms that could result. A careful check can then be kept on both the supply and use of these substances and on those employees who have access to them.

Prescribed drugs

Finally, there may be some employees taking drugs which have been prescribed by their doctors for the treatment of a specific condition. Examples include tranquillisers, sleeping tablets and drugs specifically designed to control problems such as hay fever and high blood pressure. In some instances these drugs can affect work performance. Where this puts an employee or his or her colleagues at risk, it may be necessary to arrange a transfer to different duties for a while. Examples might include those employed to operate dangerous machinery or drive vehicles. Doctors normally warn their patients about possible side effects when prescribing such drugs and employees should be encouraged to pass this information on to their managers so that appropriate adjustments can be made to workloads. Where nothing is said but a manager suspects that such drugs are being taken, some tactful investigation may be necessary.

Drink Problems

Establishing that an employee has a drink problem can be difficult. Alcoholics will not necessarily be frequently or obviously drunk. They are often highly skilled at concealing their problem and drink in such a way that no immediate effect is visible. There is also the difficulty of separating those with a drink problem from those who drink. Drinking alcohol is socially acceptable and even encouraged up to a point. Even where there are strict rules forbidding alcohol consumption in the workplace, having lunch in a pub or the company bar and meeting colleagues for a drink before going home are often part of the normal social tradition. Employees at a certain level may actually be provided with alcohol for offering to clients or colleagues when business is being discussed. Unfortunately it is all too easy for some individuals to slide from this acceptable level of drinking into alcohol dependence.

Early recognition of a drink problem is all-important. With appropriate help and rehabilitation, alcoholics can be rescued from losing their jobs and ruining their lives. Managers therefore need to be alert to the possibility of problem drinkers among their staff. The tell-tale signs are likely to be both physical and social. On the physical side, the smell of alcohol on the breath, bloodshot eyes, slurred speech, shaking hands, loss of appetite and frequent stomach upsets may all point to the problem. Social signs may include regular drinking throughout the day (although this is often carefully concealed), a deterioration in attendance, punctuality and job performance, a lowering of personal values and standards, and general changes in personality and behaviour. Affected individuals may become visibly irritable and tense (especially when deprived of alcohol) and may be noticeably less in control of their emotions than previously.

Being drunk or drinking whilst on duty will amount to serious misconduct in many workplaces and certainly where working whilst under the influence of alcohol constitutes a safety risk, eg where duties involve driving or operating machinery. In such cases the manager will need to intervene swiftly to prevent the employee from continuing work, but should beware of taking disciplinary action before investigating the situation fully. It may be revealed that the employee has an alcohol dependence problem, which needs to be treated as a matter of ill-health rather than misconduct. In this case, the employer may well be expected to help the individual overcome his or her problem. This may involve allowing time off for hospital treatment or counselling from a specialist organisation such as Alcoholics Anonymous. If the employee continues to work whilst receiving treatment, the manager will be very involved in the situation to ensure that no one is put at risk. For example, alternative duties may need to be arranged until the employee has become fully rehabilitated. It must be pointed out, however, that full rehabilitation does not always occur, and where help is refused or relapses become frequent, disciplinary action may be the only answer.

Epilepsy

Usually an employee will know if he or she suffers from epilepsy because in most cases the problem first shows itself in childhood. Provided the employee's duties and any associated risks are matched carefully with the condition and the extent to which it is successfully controlled, there is no reason why someone suffering from epilepsy should be treated differently. However, managers should know how to recognise and deal with a fit in case one occurs at work. It is advisable to have a trained first aider at the workplace and to train other staff in the basics required if a fit occurs.

The most well-known form is major epilepsy, also known as "grand mal". The person may be aware of the onset of a fit and warn those nearby. He or she will lose consciousness and usually fall down, often crying out at the same time. Parts of the body will then stiffen and twitch or shake, and the face and neck will become contorted and blue. The person may froth at the mouth and lose bladder control.

If a manager is called upon to deal with an epileptic fit, the first step is to make sure that the person is out of danger by clearing a space. Clothing should be loosened around the neck and although there is a temptation to prise the mouth open, particularly where it becomes obvious that the tongue is being bitten, this action should not be attempted. Once the convulsions have stopped the person should be laid on his or her side. The sufferer should be allowed to rest but should not be left alone until fully conscious.

It is not generally necessary for a person to go to hospital when a fit occurs, but where someone has more than one fit without regaining consciousness between them, help must be sought urgently as having repeated fits is a serious condition, which can prove fatal.

Infectious Diseases

Employers are often unsure what to do when an employee catches or comes into contact with an infectious disease. First employers must stress to their employees the importance of informing them of any infectious disease as quickly as possible. In fact, employees who work with food are required to do this by law and, in such cases, the employer must notify the local environmental health department. Even where food handling is not involved, employers have a duty under the **Health and Safety at Work, etc Act 1974** to protect their employees' health, and this includes protecting them from infectious diseases. The **Control of Substances Hazardous to Health Regulations 1994** also cover micro-organisms, eg bacteria, that may cause adverse health effects. It is therefore essential that the affected employees visit the doctor, and are not allowed to return to work before they are free from infection. In addition, the employer may wish to seek medical advice on other measures that may need to be taken in relation to the rest of the workforce.

Although the legal responsibility for reporting cases of certain infectious diseases (notifiable diseases) rests with the medical profession, employers may well wish to notify their local environmental health department of cases that are diagnosed or contacts that are reported within their workforce, to ensure that appropriate measures are taken.

HIV and AIDS

AIDS (Acquired Immune Deficiency Syndrome) is caused by a virus known as HIV (Human Immunodeficiency Virus). When a person becomes infected with this virus (ie becomes "HIV positive") it does not mean that he or she will immediately become ill with AIDS; a person may remain healthy and able to continue working for many years. However, when the condition does develop, the body starts to lose the ability to defend itself against infection. People with "full blown" AIDS often used to die as a result of their condition within a few years; however, newly developed drug therapies now enable people with AIDS to fight the virus and associated infections much more effectively and thereby prolong the length and quality of life.

It is important to realise that the virus cannot be spread through the normal day-to-day contact that occurs within the workplace, such as touching, being near someone when they speak, cough or sneeze, sharing eating and washing facilities, using toilets and working with equipment that others have used. There has to be a mix of body fluids for the virus to be transmitted and in most work situations this simply does not happen. Medical staff and first aiders will be trained to take certain precautions when dealing with an injured person, however, and it is advisable for every employee to be aware of these precautions in case they are called upon to help. The main points are:

- to cover up any cuts or abrasions of their own with waterproof plasters before treating someone else
- to avoid contact with blood by wearing gloves
- to use appropriately diluted household bleach (one part bleach to nine parts water) and disposable towels to clear up any blood spills.

Once it is known that an employee has AIDS, panic may set in among colleagues. They may refuse to work alongside the person or have any contact with him or her. Efficient work will become impossible and a resolution will have to be found. With their firsthand knowledge of the employees concerned, managers have an important part to play in reconciling the workforce.

It has to be stressed that managers are responsible for *all* their employees. They have the same obligations to a person with AIDS as they have to any other member of staff. Managers should extend to him or her the tact and sympathy which any other seriously ill person would receive.

It is to be hoped that the company will already have a policy towards people with AIDS, worked out with the employees, before the situation actually arises. This will involve giving employees a thorough understanding of how HIV can be transmitted and ensuring that first aiders routinely follow certain precautionary measures (see above). Leaflets which explain about AIDS and HIV in straightforward terms are available from a variety of sources, such as the Department of the Environment, and these could be circulated to employees to improve their understanding.

This is not to say that employees' concerns should be dismissed out of hand. Their fears are completely understandable and very real. The only way of countering these fears, however, is to present the facts in a straightforward, unemotional manner, so that anxieties are allayed in a rational way. A responsible attitude on the part of the management team will help to calm the situation. As a result of their close relationship with their subordinates, managers can provide a lead by treating an individual who is HIV positive or who has AIDS no differently from any other employee.

Legionnaires' Disease

A health problem which hits the headlines from time to time is legionnaires' disease. Although it is rare, when it does occur it can be a serious disease and in some cases fatal. It is of particular relevance to employers because the organism which causes it is typically found in water systems in large buildings such as offices and factories. Individuals may become infected by inhaling fine droplets of water which contain the bacteria. After a period of 2 to 10 days, the symptoms of high fever, chills, headache and muscle pain develop, followed by a dry cough and pneumonia. If the person is left untreated, respiratory failure and death may result.

Given the duty of every employer to protect the health and safety of his or her employees — as well as members of the public affected by the undertaking — it is important that steps should be taken to avoid outbreaks of the disease. Although it is likely that the legionella organism is present in most water systems, certain conditions must prevail before it can multiply sufficiently to become a danger. The water temperature must be within the range of 20°C to 45°C and certain nutrients, which are provided when there is sludge, scale, rust, algae or organic matter in the system, must be present. Contaminated water can only cause infection when it is dispersed into the air in droplets. So systems which do this, such as air conditioning plants with cooling towers, present the greatest risk. Avoiding legionnaires' disease has much to do with careful design and construction of water systems. How they are operated and maintained is also of crucial importance, and certain managers may be involved in regular inspection or cleaning of systems.

For most, however, responsibilities in this area will be of a general nature, such as keeping an eye open for potential dangers like an uncovered tank. Should someone be thought to have actually contracted the disease, this must be reported immediately to senior management. They in turn will contact outside bodies such as the HSE, in order to identify the source of infection and deal with the contaminated water system as quickly as possible.

Medical Suspension

As explained earlier in this chapter, those employed in certain industries or processes must be medically examined at specified intervals to ensure that their work is not jeopardising their health. Where it is felt that individuals cannot continue to work on a particular process without putting their health at risk, they may be suspended under certain regulations by an appointed doctor or an employment medical advisor for a specific or indefinite period. These regulations cover those who work with ionising radiations, lead and other hazardous substances. In some cases the employer may be in a position to offer suitable alternative work during the period of suspension but, even where this is not available, suspended employees are entitled to receive pay for up to 26 weeks provided certain qualifying conditions are met (see *Croner's Guide to Managing Absence* for full details).

Pregnancy and Maternity

In order to protect them from health and safety risks relating to pregnancy and childbirth, women are not allowed to work on certain processes in particular industries (eg indiarubber, lead and pottery). In addition, the law stipulates that all women must be given at least two weeks' leave from *any* work after giving birth. Those who work in factories must have at least four weeks.

Employers also have a duty to assess the working conditions of women of child-bearing age and new and expectant mothers in order to decide whether there are any potential health and safety risks. Risks include those to the unborn child or child of a mother who is breastfeeding as well as those to the woman herself. Categories and examples of risks include the following.

Physical Agents

- manual handling of loads
- work involving body vibration or excessive noise
- exposure to ionising radiation or extremes of temperature.

Biological Agents

- rubella, toxoplasma, hepatitis B and HIV.

Chemical Agents

- lead
- mercury
- certain pesticides.

Working Conditions

- underground mining work.

Where a risk to new or expectant mothers (ie women who are pregnant, have recently given birth or are breastfeeding) is identified, then appropriate preventative measures must be taken, as follows.

> **Pregnancy and Maternity: Steps to Safety**
>
> - Assess whether work could affect a woman who is pregnant or breastfeeding.
> - Amend work if possible to avoid risks occurring.
> - Make staff aware of the need to reassess any work that could be hazardous to a woman who is pregnant or breastfeeding.
> - Change working hours or conditions or offer suitable alternative work.
> - If neither is possible, then suspend the employee on normal pay for as long as is necessary to protect her health and safety (ss.66–68 of the **Employment Rights Act 1996**).

Night Work

Special consideration needs to be given to new and expectant mothers who work at night. Where such an employee has a medical certificate which says that night work could affect her health and safety, then the employer must either offer her suitable alternative work where it is available, or give her paid leave for as long as is necessary to protect her health and safety.

Rest Facilities

Under the **Workplace (Health, Safety and Welfare) Regulations 1992**, pregnant and breastfeeding employees must be provided with suitable facilities to rest (see page 119).

6 The Inspector Calls

It is probably true to say that a visit from the health and safety inspector is not often greeted with wild enthusiasm by a company. In fact, the reverse may well be the case. One reason for this is that inspectors are frequently perceived to cause trouble and nuisance and only find things for the company to spend money on. Some may have had negative experiences with inspectors in the past, which makes them unlikely to welcome subsequent visiting inspectors with open arms. But bad feelings towards inspectors are often based on misunderstanding, about who they are, what they are appointed to do, what they *can* do and how they generally go about doing it.

Managers may be inclined to feel that inspectors should deal only with those who have overall responsibility for health and safety in the company, which does not involve them. Most managers would not be in a position to deal with a health and safety inspector directly and would not be required to do so.The inspector would normally be referred to the safety officer, company secretary, a senior manager, or the personnel department. However, a situation may arise where the manager is the most senior or most appropriate person on the premises at the time. For instance, the inspector may arrive outside normal office hours, or the person he or she needs to see may not be available. In such circumstances, knowing something about the role of inspectors and their rights will make it easier for the manager to deal with them. Also, as explained below, inspectors have the legal power to interview any person they think necessary in the exercise of their responsibilites. All staff with responsibility for greeting visitors (eg reception, security gates) should be given written directions on the correct procedure for the arrival of HSE inspectors if an inspection is unannounced.

The Enforcing Authorities

The Health and Safety Executive (HSE) is responsible overall for enforcing health and safety legislation, but there are particular "enforcing authorities" who actually have the power of enforcement and who carry it out in practice. The HSE itself is the main enforcing authority, but there are certain types of premises for which the local authority (ie local district council or London borough) is the enforcing authority. In particular, the local authority is responsible for most offices, hotels, pubs, restaurants and shops, together with many leisure premises.

Both the HSE and the local authority are responsible for appointing suitably qualified inspectors whose main purpose is to ensure that the law on health and safety is complied with.

The Inspector's Powers

In order to ensure that the law on health and safety is upheld, inspectors have the power, as long as they are acting within their field of responsibility, to do any of the following:

- enter any premises at any reasonable time (or at any time if they believe a situation to be dangerous)
- require a police officer, or anyone else authorised by the enforcing authority, to accompany them if they believe they are likely to be obstructed
- bring with them any equipment or materials
- inspect the premises
- carry out any examination or investigation they consider necessary, including taking measurements, photographs or any other kind of recording
- order that the premises be left undisturbed while they carry out the investigation

- take samples of anything found on the premises, or have it dismantled or tested
- demand to be shown any book or document they consider necessary, not just those which have to be kept by law
- require the use of facilities (such as an office) or obtain any help and assistance they feel they might need
- interview and ask questions of anyone they consider appropriate, either alone or in the presence of any other person whom the inspector has invited or allowed to be present; the person being interviewed may be required to sign a declaration of the truth of his or her answers.

Finally, if this does not cover all their requirements, inspectors are also granted — by law — any other power which is necessary for them to enforce the law.

Generally, any improvements or changes that inspectors consider necessary are likely to be discussed at the time of their visit. The requirements may then be confirmed in writing, and inspectors may even indicate that they will be coming back to check on certain matters. At this stage, inspectors do not have the power to require any changes to be made. It is reasonable to suppose, however, that if the remedial action they indicated by discussion and letter has not been taken by the time they return, then some sort of enforcement action with legal backing *will* be taken. In some cases the preliminary informal warnings described above may not take place. Legally, inspectors can exercise any of their powers without giving a warning, although the normal practice is to use persuasion before enforcement. Where enforcement action is taken it is initially in the form of either an improvement or a prohibition notice.

Improvement and Prohibition Notices

These notices can be served by inspectors on the spot when they make a visit. There is no need to apply to a court for permission to serve one or to await a prosecution.

Improvement notice
This may be served by inspectors if they believe that a person has broken and/or is breaking one or more of the relevant statutory provisions regarding health and safety and it seems likely that the contravention will be continued or repeated. This covers anything from the general provisions of the **Health and Safety at Work, etc Act 1974** to the specific requirements of the **Factories Act 1961** or the **Offices, Shops and Railway Premises Act 1963**. In the improvement notice inspectors must:

- state that they believe the law has been broken
- specify precisely which statutory provision they believe has been breached
- give detailed reasons for holding this view
- specify a period of time (not less than 21 days) in which the employer is expected to remedy the situation.

Note that the improvement notice does not have to tell the employer *how* to put things right, though it might include instructions on what should be done by the employer, possibly referring to a code of practice. Alternatively, inspectors may give more informal advice either during their visit or subsequently.

Prohibition notice
This may be served by inspectors who believe that an activity is going on which involves or will involve a risk of serious personal injury. In the prohibition notice inspectors must:

- state their belief regarding the risk of serious personal injury
- specify what creates the risk in question
- state their belief that an actual or potential breach of statutory provisions is involved (where this is the case), giving reasons

- direct that the unsafe practice or activity must not continue.

The prohibition notice differs from the improvement notice in a number of ways. To begin with it does not *have* to refer to breaches of specific health and safety provisions. A prohibition notice can be served anywhere an inspector considers there to be a hazardous practice or situation. The important thing is that a serious personal injury risk has been identified. In addition, a prohibition notice can take effect immediately, whereas the improvement notice gives the employer time to put things right. The prohibition notice may require the hazardous activity to be stopped immediately, or it may be what is called a "deferred prohibition notice", in which case it will specify a time-limit after which the hazardous activity must stop unless the risk has been removed.

Anyone who has had an improvement or prohibition notice served against them can appeal to an industrial tribunal, as long as they do so within 21 days of it being served. An appeal against an improvement notice means that it is automatically suspended until the appeal has been heard or withdrawn. However, an appeal against a prohibition notice will result in its suspension only if that is ordered by the tribunal.

Prosecution

If all else fails, inspectors may institute prosecution proceedings. If prosecution is being considered this is usually made clear in advance and an opportunity is given for a meeting between the inspector concerned and a senior person in the company. Managers should be aware, therefore, that they might receive the advance warning concerning prosecution on behalf of the company. It is important to pass it on to the appropriate level of management immediately.

Some of the main offences for which companies or individuals can be prosecuted in respect of health and safety are:

- failing to comply with an improvement or prohibition notice
- obstructing inspectors in the course of their duties
- failing to carry out any of the general duties of the **Health and Safety at Work, etc Act 1974** or other relevant statutes
- breaching any health and safety regulations
- making a false statement or entry in a register, document, etc required to be kept by law.

A person who contravenes an improvement or prohibition notice may be liable, on summary conviction (ie before magistrates), to a fine of up to £20,000 or a six month prison sentence or both. Conviction on indictment (ie before a jury) can result in an unlimited fine and/or up to two years' imprisonment. Most offences involving the obstruction of inspectors in the exercise of their powers are dealt with summarily, and the maximum penalty in such circumstances is £5000.

All managers should note that it is not just the employer who is liable to prosecution. Employees and members of management who are involved in an offence may also be prosecuted. Additionally, an act or omission of any employee which is apparently condoned by the company (eg by the manager failing to take corrective action) will make the company liable for prosecution.

The Manager's Role

What are the implications of inspectors' rights and powers for managers, and how should they deal with visiting inspectors?

First, the operation of any policy of non-co-operation by managers would be extremely unwise. However undesirable an inspector's presence on the premises, there is no point in trying to refuse entry. (It must be remembered that obstructing an inspector is a criminal offence.) It is permissible, however, to ask inspectors for their visiting card, which they should carry with them, and for proof of their powers, which they should also be able to produce. Once their identity has been checked, it is perfectly reasonable to ask an inspector to wait until a more senior person can be contacted and has arrived. Most inspectors will be happy to do this. However, if they suspect that something the company does not want seen is being removed from sight while they wait, they may insist on inspecting the premises immediately.

Whatever happens, where a manager is the most senior person on the premises, it is important that he or she accompanies the inspector at all times (or at least as much as the inspector will allow). There are some situations in which managers can insist on being present — these include the dismantling or testing of anything on the premises. Also, where inspectors exercise their powers to take a sample of any substance on the premises, they must leave a similar sample with a manager (or other responsible person) or provide written confirmation that a sample has been taken. Another good reason for managers accompanying inspectors whenever possible is that, should the inspector's action result in any damage to the company's property or business, they can be sued for damages (which, in practice, the enforcing authority will generally cover). A manager who is present can be a useful witness to the fact that it was the inspector's actions which caused the damage.

Giving Statements

A manager may be worried about the implications of making any sort of statement to an inspector or of allowing others to do so. There is a statutory obligation to give a statement if required, but it is not admissible as evidence in court proceedings against the individual who makes it. Therefore it is not possible for people to incriminate themselves by what they say. In fact it is likely to be their refusal to say anything which could make them liable to prosecution, ie for obstructing an inspector in the carrying out of his or her duties. Where inspectors wish to use what an individual says in court proceedings against that person, they must caution the individual as the police do.

In such circumstances the individual does *not* have to say anything and may wish to consult a solicitor. Other than where a caution has been given, refusing to make a statement or advising others to do so is not a sensible approach. Whilst such action might be viewed as an act of loyalty to the company, it is exposing the individual concerned to the risk of prosecution.

At the End of the Visit

Having completed an investigation, the inspector is under an obligation to provide certain information. It is an inspector's duty to supply employees and/or their safety representatives with the following:

- factual information obtained during the visit
- notices of prosecution
- copies of correspondence, improvement or prohibition notices issued to the employer
- details of any action the inspector proposes to take as a result of the visit.

Whenever such information is given it must also be provided to the employer, or to his or her representative, ie the manager. The situation should not arise where the safety representative knows more than the manager as a result of an inspector's visit.

Managers should make as detailed notes as possible of what inspectors say and do during their visits. It is particularly important to be able to pass on to senior management any informal warnings which inspectors give and which might be seen as forerunners to legal enforcement if ignored. Such notes might also provide vital evidence of occasions where inspectors have failed to exercise their powers properly. It is also worth finding out what an inspector plans to do as a result of a visit — if this has not already been made clear. It may be appropriate to ask whether the inspector will be writing to the company, returning to check on things again soon (and if so, when) or taking any other action. Essentially a manager needs to be in a position to make a full report on the visit to senior management.

Take a Positive View

Having highlighted the negative aspects of inspectors' visits it needs to be acknowledged that, in many cases, inspectors can make a worthwhile and positive contribution to the company. Many employers see them as advisors to whom they can turn for help to solve health and safety problems. They often have considerable experience of the problems faced by employers and can offer new ideas and suggest solutions gleaned from their visits to other employers and workplaces. They can also provide an important objective viewpoint, identifying dangers, risks, etc which have not been recognised by those in the company because of long and close involvement with particular processes, work methods, etc. In most cases inspectors will first attempt to rectify dangerous situations by persuasion and discussion. Only if this fails to have the desired effect, or where the situation is more serious, will they resort to improvement or prohibition notices, and then only if these are ignored is prosecution likely to result.

7 Problem Areas

While specific industries have their own particular hazards, there are certain problems which are common to all types of occupation and organisation. The health and safety policy will set out management responsibilities in respect of the health and safety of employees, and managers must be clear about where their own responsibilities lie. When considering the problem areas outlined in this chapter it will be clear that managers have a major role to play in preventing hazards or in dealing with the difficulties which arise.

The emphasis throughout is on the importance of adequate training, supervision and monitoring. The manager is the person best placed to assess the capabilities of employees within the department and this assessment should be put to use when formulating safe practices and procedures.

Maintaining the Workplace

The essential starting point for a working environment that is healthy and safe is a policy of "good housekeeping". Taking the same care of our workplaces as we do of our homes would prevent many accidents occurring.

Unfortunately, few people treat their workplace with the same respect and on a day-to-day basis it is left to the manager to ensure that employees recognise potential hazards, take steps to avoid their occurrence or, at least, report them automatically.

Maintaining the Workplace Under the Workplace (Health, Safety and Welfare) Regulations 1992
These regulations apply to all workplaces (except where an employee is working in his or her own home when the responsibility will rest primarily with the employee) and require employers to maintain the workplace and work equipment in:

- an efficient state
- efficient working order, and
- good repair.

The Approved Code of Practice (ACOP) which goes with the regulations provides detailed advice on how this should be done. It identifies certain items that can be properly maintained only through setting up suitable systems consisting of regular checks, tests, remedial action and record keeping. Examples of such items include safety equipment, emergency lighting and fencing to machinery.

The regulations also require that:

- the workplace, furniture and fittings are kept sufficiently clean
- waste materials are not allowed to accumulate in the workplace except in suitable receptacles, and
- floors are kept free from articles and substances likely to cause slips, trips and falls.

Many people associate accidents at work with machinery but, even in factories, more accidents are caused by slips and falls or bumping into objects than by machinery.

About one-fifth of accidents at work involve slips, trips or other falls. Managers should be aware of the type of surface people are walking on and whether it is suitable for the activity being carried out. In addition they should check that the treatment and maintenance of that surface is appropriate. Damaged or uneven surfaces can be lethal and should be clearly signposted as a hazard until they can be repaired.

Changes to levels in the flooring, such as a small step between departments, need to be adequately lit to avoid people tripping. Staircases also need good lighting, together with sturdy handrails and anti-slip tread.

A procedure for reporting and dealing with spillages of liquids or greasy substances is also important. No one should assume that someone else has reported a cup of coffee spilt on the stairs. The manager may also be responsible for areas outside the building, such as a yard or pedestrian access route, and these should not be forgotten. Icy surfaces in winter, for example, will need grit and salt.

It may be the case that because of the inherent dangers, specified footwear must be worn at all times by the workforce. If so, managers will be responsible for monitoring compliance and disciplining those who fail to follow the company's rules.

Obstructions and badly placed furniture and equipment can also cause accidents in the workplace. Effective housekeeping will guarantee that boxes, heaps of papers and files, etc are not left in corridors or walkways, that sharp corners of cabinets or desks are not likely to jab the unwary and that drawers are always closed after use. Heaps of materials should be stacked safely so that they are not likely to fall on the innocent passer-by. Trailing telephone wires and leads from electrical equipment need to be sited out of harm's way or adequately covered.

Good housekeeping, more than any other aspect of health and safety management, is a matter of common sense. However, since the workforce cannot always be relied upon to act in a sensible manner, managers need to carry out regular inspections in their area to maintain a clean and tidy environment.

To summarise, areas which require constant attention are as follows.

Checklist: Good Housekeeping

- damaged floor coverings
- uneven surfaces
- slippery surfaces
- worn treads on stairs
- staircase handrails missing or damaged
- trailing cables
- obstructions in pedestrian walkways and corridors
- poor lighting
- protruding corners on cabinets, desks or benches
- overloaded cabinets
- windows on swing doors obscured
- waste material lying around
- materials poorly stacked.

Fire

Since major fires occur rarely, people tend to become blasé about fire precautions and assume that, even if a fire started, they would be able to get out of the building before the flames and smoke overtook them. It is in this complacency that danger lies and managers must play a major role in keeping employees alert to the threat of fire. Employees must be under no illusions about the effects of smoke and fire. Fire spreads rapidly and the associated smoke and fumes quickly overcome anyone in their path.

Under the **Workplace (Fire Precautions) Regulations 1997** all workplaces must be assessed for fire hazards and suitable controls put in place. In addition, all factory, office and shop premises where more than 20 people normally work or where more than 10 people work other than on the ground floor require a fire certificate. So too do other premises such as hotels in which sleeping accommodation is provided and buildings in which large quantities of flammable material or explosives are stored. The fire certificate will set out various requirements including the means of escape to be provided, the maintenance and freedom from obstruction of the escape routes, fire-fighting apparatus, warning systems and the training of employees.

Within the requirements imposed by the certificate the organisation will set up procedures for safe evacuation, maintenance of fire-fighting equipment and so on. The first task of a manager in this connection is to become thoroughly familiar both with instructions to be followed in the event of a fire and with precautionary measures to prevent such an occurrence. The second task is to ensure that other employees are also fully briefed.

Elementary steps can be taken to minimise the risk of fire as indicated in the checklist overleaf.

A physical check of the workplace every night is strongly advised.

To facilitate escape and prevent the spread of fire, further precautions need to be taken. Employees should know what their escape route is and this route should be kept free from obstructions. Fire exits must be kept clearly marked and easy to open while people are on the premises. Consideration should be given to the arrangement of every workroom so that there is a free passageway to a fire exit. Fire doors must not be wedged open.

If a fire drill has not been held for years, there can be no guarantee that fire evacuation procedures set down on paper work effectively in practice. The line manager should draw this fact to the attention of more senior management.

Should a small fire break out, employees may be tempted to handle it themselves by using the fire-fighting equipment. If there is the slightest danger that the flames will not be doused in this way, the attempt should not be made. Two individuals should always be present at such attempts.

Checklist: Fire Precautions

- Require smokers to use ashtrays rather than waste bins or the floor.
- Place portable heaters in safe positions where they cannot be overturned accidentally and *never* allow them to be used for drying tea towels. They should always stand securely on a non-combustible surface, well away from debris of any kind. These should not be used unless absolutely no other form of heating is reasonably practicable.
- Ensure COSHH assessment of all substances have covered fire risks and suitable controls are in place.
- Regularly check electrical equipment and gas appliances (as required under various health and safety regulations).
- Remove combustible material from areas where it is not needed.
- Ensure that refuse is disposed of quickly.
- Correctly store and use flammable liquids (including typewriter correction fluid).
- Ban smoking from store rooms where such articles are kept.
- Turn off electrical equipment overnight.

Fire Extinguishers

There are different types of fire extinguisher to use depending on the type of fire involved, eg water extinguishers should be used only for ordinary combustible fires whereas carbon dioxide extinguishers can also be used for fires involving electrical equipment. It is important that anyone who may have to use such fire-fighting equipment understands fully which extinguisher is to be used in which circumstance.

Procedures and Prevention

When the fire alarm rings, there may be a moment of disbelief followed by some panic. At this time the supervising manager must exert a calming influence to ensure an orderly and complete evacuation. Staff should not be allowed to retrieve belongings if this means that a delay will occur; neither should they use lifts.

Once managers know and understand what is involved in the prevention of fire they must ensure that their subordinates appreciate the important points.

First, employees should be made aware of company or departmental rules which aim to prevent the outbreak of fire (eg no naked flames near flammable vapours, smokers must use ashtrays, etc), and know that they will be disciplined if they fail to comply.

Second, they should be made fully conversant with procedures to be followed in the event of fire. These procedures should be clear and precise and translated into any languages used by ethnic minority members of the workforce, where necessary. Furthermore the instructions should be regularly updated to take into account any office moves, or re-siting of dangerous machinery, etc. Everyone should know his or her role when a fire occurs and special arrangements should cover disabled employees and visitors to the premises. All procedures should take into account the fact that at any given time those with particular responsibilities may be away because of sickness, holidays, etc.

Noise

Under the **Noise at Work Regulations 1989**, in situations where there is a daily noise exposure of at least 85dB(A) over a working day, employers have to assess the noise, inform their employees and issue personal ear protection to those who request it. At a daily exposure of 90dB(A) and above, they must reduce noise where reasonably practicable, designate ear protection zones and ensure that employees wear ear protectors when entering those zones.

So, the employer's first responsibility is to try to keep noise levels down as much as possible. This means seeing that enclosures and silencers are routinely kept in position during the operation of noisy machinery. Managers should also encourage employees to report any defect in such equipment as soon as it is spotted and should welcome any suggestions for improvements.

Where, despite such efforts, noise is such that employees must wear ear plugs or ear muffs (either because of the regulations or because employers consider it wise even at a lower noise level), it should be made clear that failure to do so will be considered a disciplinary offence.

The second responsibility placed on employers by the regulations is to inform employees about the risk of damage to hearing that noise levels at work represent and the steps that should be taken to minimise that risk. Managers may well be involved in this, both by formal training and by giving general guidance on a day-to-day basis.

High noise levels necessarily mean that normal sounds, such as people shouting warnings, go unheard. It is therefore sensible for managers to devise procedures which cover such situations adequately, for instance by requiring a positive response from the person spoken to in acknowledgement that the warning has been heard. Otherwise there will be a significant risk of accidents.

Whilst employers are not legally required to have their employees' hearing checked, arranging tests or encouraging employees to go for these is likely to be part of a responsible company's way of ensuring high standards of health and safety where there is exposure to significant levels of noise at work.

Electricity

We can all take electricity too much for granted, sometimes with fatal results. Accidents in the home caused by faulty wiring, damaged cables or overloaded circuits occur frequently. Even in the best run working establishments, where regular maintenance of all electrical equipment is carried out meticulously, some factors can still threaten safety. For example, in an effort to improve the office facilities an employee may bring in a kettle from home, only to find that it does not work properly because it has faulty wiring which nearly causes a fire.

Electricity cannot be seen and this is one of the reasons that it is necessary to spell out to people the hazards associated with it. Danger of electric shock and severe burning arises from ignorance and carelessness.

Electrical safety in the workplace is governed by the **Electricity at Work Regulations 1989**, which require the testing of equipment by competent persons (and more generally by the **Management of Health and Safety at Work Regulations 1992**). These require employers to assess work activities which use (or may be affected by) electricity, to decide whether there is risk of injury and to take appropriate action.

Under the regulations, all electrical equipment and systems must be suitable and safe. Care must be taken, therefore, in choosing, installing and maintaining equipment, and in insulating and earthing electrical systems. In doing all this, employers must take full account of manufacturers' instructions and recommendations. Where electrical equipment is actually operated, adequate space around it and access to it must be provided, and the area must be properly lit.

Particular attention must be given to work on any part of an electrical circuit. Wherever possible, work should start only after the system has been rendered "dead". Work on a live system is only permissible if it is *not* reasonable for it to be rendered dead first and it *is* reasonable for the work to be carried out in the circumstances. Even then all other possible steps must be taken to minimise the risk of injury. In any event, only competent persons may work on a live system and only authorised persons should be allowed anywhere near the proceedings.

Whilst the regulations place the major burden of responsibility for electrical safety on employers, employees also have a duty to meet the various requirements in areas within their control, as well as helping their employers fulfil their duties. This means that managers will be very much involved on a practical day-to-day basis in ensuring a safe workplace. Indeed, a manager may well be the "competent person" for risk assessment purposes under the **Management of Health and Safety at Work Regulations 1992** (see page 8).

The starting point for electrical safety is the appropriate care and maintenance of equipment. If there are any worries at all about the possibility of its being defective, the equipment should be disconnected until it is repaired. Some common faults are:

- loose connections
- poor insulation
- exposed wires
- damaged leads
- broken switches
- overloaded circuits.

Employees should be told that they must report all possible faults and must never plug in extra equipment unless they are authorised to do so. On no account should electrical items be brought from home for use at work unless express permission has been given. If an item is thought to be faulty it should be removed, if possible, from its normal location and locked away until it can be mended. When a faulty piece of equipment cannot be moved it should be clearly labelled as defective and where possible rendered inoperable. Employees should be informed that it must not be used.

Portable electrical apparatus can present special hazards. Sometimes the equipment is infrequently used and therefore poorly maintained; on the other hand cables can become worn through excessive use and circuits can be overloaded by tools being thoughtlessly plugged in. Precautions need to be taken to minimise the hazards and for such tools it is advisable to use a residual current circuit breaker.

Most people are aware that it is foolish to mix electricity and water and would not dream of risking this in the home. Common sense does not always extend to the workplace, however, and it is advisable to remind employees about the dangers of leaving liquids which can be knocked over on top of electric typewriters, computer terminals, photocopiers, etc. In addition, touching electrical apparatus with wet hands must be outlawed.

At any workplace it is vital that all employees are constantly reminded of and trained in good safety practice in relation to electricity and electrical machinery and equipment. The consequences, otherwise, can be disastrous.

Machinery

Machines of all kinds — guillotines, power presses, moving belts, drills, etc — present a host of hazards in the workplace. The work that many machines are required to do makes them intrinsically dangerous. Employees may be injured by part of their body or clothing becoming trapped in the machinery, by being struck by moving parts of the machinery or hit by flying particles. Because the machine cannot do its job without presenting these dangers, steps must be taken to protect the employee from the machine by fencing, guards and other safety devices. It is the employer's duty to provide and maintain plant and systems of work that are safe, including the guarding of machines and their safe siting.

From 1 January 1997, every aspect of the use of equipment at work is governed by the **Provision and Use of Work Equipment Regulations 1992.**

The general requirements of the regulations (applicable to all equipment — see below) specify that any equipment provided for work must be suitable for its intended use and must be properly maintained. Any equipment which poses a specific risk to health and safety must only be used and maintained by designated employees who have been properly trained.

Provision and Use of Work Equipment Regulations 1992

These regulations consist of two sets of requirements.

General requirements — these are concerned with:

- maintenance
- suitability
- information
- instructions
- training
- EU conformity.

Specific requirements — these are concerned with:

- dangerous parts
- protection against specified hazards
- temperature extremes
- control systems
- power isolation
- stability
- lighting
- maintenance
- markings and warnings.

There is a general requirement under the **Factories Act 1961** and the **Offices, Shops and Railway Premises Act 1963** for the dangerous parts of all machinery to be securely fenced. The fencing must be of stout construction and must be regularly maintained. Fencing may be removed only for lubrication or adjustment and that work may be performed only by people over the age of 18. There are specific requirements under the **Factories Act 1961** relating to the fencing of prime movers (engines) and transmission machinery.

Where dangerous parts of machinery cannot be fenced because it would make the machine's operation impossible, guards must be supplied to prevent the operator coming into contact with the dangerous parts. The **Provision and Use of Work Equipment Regulations 1992**, as part of their "specific" requirements (see box on previous page) refer to the "danger zones" around machinery in which people are at risk of being harmed through contact with dangerous parts. Under the **Provision and Use of Work Equipment Regulations 1992**, employers must take appropriate measures to prevent access to these dangerous parts, or must stop them moving before people enter the danger zone.

Apart from the general duty to fence or guard, there are also more specific requirements relating to items of plant and machinery in specified industries. An example is the woodworking industry, where numerous items such as different kinds of saws, planing machines, trenching machines and certain lathes are listed as inherently dangerous and therefore require guards or fencing.

It is obvious that those most at risk from dangerous machinery are young and/or inexperienced employees and those who are inadequately trained or supervised. In recognition of the danger to the young, legislation provides that certain machines in factories may not be operated by young people unless they are fully trained and supervised. The list includes the following (when worked with mechanical power): dough mixers, brick and tile presses, certain machines used in laundries, meat mincing machines, pie and tart making machines, semi-automatic wood turning lathes, etc. Guillotines and platen printing machines are also included, whether they are power operated or not. In addition, the **Health and Safety (Young Persons) Regulations**

1997 require any risks to young persons to be assessed, taking into account the young person's inexperience, immaturity and lack of awareness of risks.

Similar provisions apply to dangerous machinery used in offices and shops. Here, however, the legislation states that no one, regardless of age, may work on certain machines unless they have received full instruction and adequate training and are supervised by someone with knowledge and experience of the machines. Many of the machines listed are the same as itemised for factories but also include circular knife slicing machines used for bacon, etc, potato chipping machines, wrapping and packing machines and various others.

With the emphasis on instructing employees, training and control, managers will be very much involved with the safety of the machines within their departments.

Managers themselves must be fully conversant with the dangers involved. Every potential hazard connected with the machines under their control should be identified, including those which may arise through thoughtless or careless behaviour. With this clearly in mind managers need to set up a system to ensure that safeguarding devices are properly maintained and *always* used. Guards must be checked regularly and a reporting system instituted to bring faults or wear and tear to the manager's notice. Many accidents are caused when employees operate machines without their proper guards attached. It has to be stressed to all concerned that *whatever* the circumstances, no machine may be operated without its guard. To do so will be considered a disciplinary offence.

An awareness of, and healthy respect for, dangerous machinery on the part of the manager will provide the lead to other members of the department. Any negligent, thoughtless or careless behaviour near the machines must be disciplined if the safety precautions are to be taken seriously. Before anyone is allowed to operate such machinery the manager must be completely satisfied that he or she has received proper instruction in its operation (an operating manual should always be left close by), is fully trained to cope with a non-routine occurrence (such as machine breakdown) and is adequately supervised by someone with thorough knowledge of that particular machine. The same considerations will apply to long-standing members of the department who are asked to work on a machine with which they are not familiar.

In case of accidents, all employees should know how the machine is turned off and where the switch for the electrical supply is located.

Supply of Machinery

Most machinery supplied or imported in the UK must now comply with the **Supply of Machinery (Safety) Regulations 1992**. This means that it must meet certain essential health and safety requirements in relation to, for example, moving parts, controls, fire, noise, emissions, maintenance and instructions. It must undergo a conformity assessment procedure, be issued with various certificates, and carry a "CE" mark before it can be supplied.

Fork-lift Trucks

Every year in this country there are many thousands of reportable accidents, some fatal, involving fork-lift trucks. Accidents not only cause suffering and anguish to the injured employees and their relatives but create a significant cost to the company in terms of damage to plant and equipment.

Campaigns have been launched in an effort to make managers realise the seriousness of the situation because, as in virtually all aspects of health and safety management, it is the manager in the factory or warehouse who can influence significantly the safe use of this equipment.

There are no statutory provisions specifically relating to fork-lift trucks but there is a helpful HSE guidance booklet (Booklet HS(G)6 *Safety in working with lift trucks*) and an approved code of practice on fork-lift training produced by the Health and Safety Commission.

Employees should not be permitted to drive a fork-lift truck unless they have been adequately trained and are authorised to do so, or alternatively are receiving formal training under supervision. The selection of suitable drivers is most important. Reliability and maturity, together with mental and physical fitness, are essential character traits. Where the medical aspects are concerned, a driver should have full body movement, good eyesight and hearing, and a calm disposition. Never choose someone whose health is questionable or who is emotionally disturbed.

Training is stressed again and again. The trainers themselves should be fully experienced in the particular tasks to be undertaken by the trainees. There are three stages to training:

- impartation of basic skills and knowledge (the code of practice provides practical guidance on how this should be done)
- specific job training in a safe area to develop the skills required
- familiarisation training in the actual workplace.

In addition to learning how to operate the truck, employees must be taught its dangers and limitations. Accidents are frequently caused by speeding, with gangways, entrances and exits being particularly unsafe. Overloading, too, is not uncommon and each vehicle should have its safe working capacity displayed on it.

On a day-to-day basis managers have the responsibility for seeing that operators are properly trained and are working safely. Clearly this means that regular and routine checks need to be made by managers and a procedure must be established for reporting any faults or near accidents.

Simple rules for operating trucks should be made known to all drivers, and preferably displayed in a prominent place so that no one can claim ignorance. Such rules would include the following, suggested by the HSE.

Checklist: Operating Fork-lift Trucks

- If you are not well, don't drive. Report to the manager.
- Take extra care when pedestrians are about.
- Always sound the horn at all danger spots.
- Never brake violently other than in an emergency.
- Do not run over cables on the floor unless they are properly protected.
- Never leave the truck unattended on a slope.
- Always immobilise the machine when not in use and secure the keys, etc.

Lifting and Carrying

There are many situations at work where the lifting and carrying of loads can put employees at risk. In fact, more than a quarter of all injuries at work each year are caused by "manual handling". The **Manual Handling Operations Regulations 1992** are specific regulations governing this area of health and safety, and employers must ensure that the problem is properly addressed.

The regulations require that, as far as possible, employees should not be asked, or allowed, to transport or handle loads in such a way as could injure them. Where the task is unavoidable, then the employer must assess the risks involved and reduce them to the lowest possible level.

Definitions from the Manual Handling Operations Regulations 1992
"Manual handling operations" means any transporting or supporting of a load by hand or bodily force, and includes lifting, putting down, pushing, pulling, carrying or moving.
"Load" means any item or object that is being transported or supported.

With the regulations now established in the workplace, managers are ideally placed for helping their employers identify and assess the risks associated with lifting and carrying, and for helping them find solutions to the problems identified. With a little thought, it may be possible to actually eliminate some handling procedures altogether. For example, it may be possible to deliver goods to the point of use or to carry out a task *in situ* rather than elsewhere. Introducing machinery to do the lifting and carrying or providing help in the form of hoists or trolleys may be the answer. In other situations, quite simple changes may be sufficient. For example, splitting the load, involving more employees, or providing gloves or handgrips.

Consideration should also be given to the individual capabilities of those involved. For example, some employees may be more susceptible to injury than others as a result of age, medical history or pregnancy.

Managers need to take a long hard look at the working environment and ask themselves whether there are any changes which need to be made. For instance, there may be so little room for manoeuvre that employees have no choice but to lift loads awkwardly, or a movement which is normally safe may become dangerous because of a wet floor or an unreplaced light bulb.

Finally, employees need to be trained in how to handle and move loads safely, and how to use lifting equipment to their best advantage.

Visual Display Units (VDUs)

The last 20 years have seen an explosion in the use of VDUs and other display screen equipment (DSE) in the workplace. As with any new technology it takes a while for employees to accustom themselves to the requirements of the new machines and it is understandable that problems have arisen in connection with their use. Nevertheless, there is now general agreement that health hazards arising from the operation of VDUs can largely be eliminated.

At the beginning of 1993, the **Health and Safety (Display Screen Equipment) Regulations 1992** were introduced. These apply not only to conventional VDUs but also to non-electronic systems such as microfiche and production process control panels. Most screen equipment which displays text, numbers or graphics is covered by the regulations, although there are certain exceptions, such as calculators, cash registers and window typewriters.

The regulations require employers to take certain measures to protect the health and safety of DSE users. These are people who habitually use DSE as a significant part of their normal work. The most often quoted test of user status is an hour or more on most working days.

Workstations

Each individual workstation must be assessed in order to establish whether it poses any health and safety risks, for example postural or visual problems, and likelihood of stress or fatigue. A workstation is defined as the combination of the personal computer, monitor, keyboard, chair, desk and other equipment.

Equipment

All workstations must comply with certain minimum requirements. These include the following:

- equipment must be adjustable
- screen must be glare-free

- lighting, temperature and humidity must be appropriate.

Work Breaks

The daily routine of DSE users must be arranged so that their work is periodically interrupted either by breaks or by changes in activity. If possible, jobs should consist of a variety of tasks, but where long periods of screen work are unavoidable, then regular breaks are essential. Short frequent breaks are more useful than longer infrequent ones.

Eyesight

DSE users are entitled to appropriate eye and eyesight tests both before they embark on DSE work and at regular intervals thereafter. Employers must pay for these tests and for any spectacles which are provided to correct vision defects for DSE work.

Training

DSE users must receive proper information and training about the health and safety risks associated with their work and the measures they must take to ensure that they remain fit and healthy.

Many organisations have detailed policies and procedures (sometimes drawn up in conjunction with recognised trade unions) covering various aspects of working with DSE. Managers should ensure that guidelines and rules contained in company policies are followed, for example by insisting that rest breaks are taken at the intervals specified. In this way many problems can be avoided.

In general the most common complaints arising from DSE operation are:

- eye strain and headaches
- mental and physical fatigue
- musculoskeletal problems (eg upper limb disorders)
- general stress.

By complying with the new regulations, many of these problems can be avoided or solved. For instance, the correct lighting will reduce glare, so exterior windows should have blinds, especially if direct sunlight enters the room. Eye tests for potential DSE users will identify possible problems with eye strain, and regular eye tests thereafter will reassure people that their eyesight is not deteriorating. Bodily and mental fatigue will be alleviated by breaks in DSE operation.

The positioning of desk, chair and workstation in relation to each other is important. Chairs should be adjustable in height and have movable back rests, footrests should be supplied and desks should be high enough for the operators to get their legs underneath in comfort.

Less common complaints which have been mentioned in connection with DSE include:

- facial dermatitis
- risk of experiencing an epileptic fit following exposure to a flickering light source.

The latter occurs only among the small percentage of people prone to photosensitive epilepsy and such individuals should be referred for medical opinion before being asked to work on VDUs. Facial dermatitis has been linked to low humidity and static electricity around the VDU. Anti-static carpeting and humidifying devices should help. Advice may be obtained from the local Employment Medical Advisory Service (EMAS).

Perhaps the most difficult problem to handle in relation to VDUs is reluctance on the part of a pregnant employee to continue working with one. Over recent years, there has been much speculation over whether DSE emissions can cause miscarriages or birth defects. The latest advice from the HSE is that there is no causal link, and that there is no need for pregnant women to stop working with DSE. It is recognised, however, that worry and anxiety themselves can cause difficulties in pregnancy, and employees in this position should be handled with tact and sympathy.

If a woman approaches a manager and asks to be taken off DSE duties for the duration of her pregnancy, she should be given the opportunity to discuss her concerns with someone who has up-to-date medical knowledge on the subject. The likely issues that have relevance to pregnancy will be to ensure good posture, back and leg support and that rest breaks are provided.

If she is still insistent her request may have to be referred to more senior management for approval. Nevertheless, a manager's understanding attitude to the woman's dilemma and a willingness to consider a reduction in hours worked on a VDU or a temporary transfer to another job will often help resolve the problem satisfactorily.

Where agency workers are used in the workplace, the agency has a duty to train them and provide eyesight tests, but the host organisation must ensure the provision of adequate adjustable equipment. Home-based employees using DSE have to be assessed by issuing a risk assessment checklist for them to complete and to be provided with the required equipment. Home-based employees should also be provided with eyesight tests.

Dangerous Substances

It has always been the case that in some industries the very nature of the work means that employees regularly work with substances or agents which may have hazardous properties. It is the duty of the employer to minimise, as far as is reasonably practicable, the risk presented to employees whilst working with such substances or agents.

Extensive regulations cover operations in these areas and all responsible companies will have thorough training and refresher programmes geared to promote safe working in the light of the relevant legislation.

However, under the **Control of Substances Hazardous to Health Regulations 1994** *every* employer has a responsibility to assess the risks associated with hazardous substances in the workplace and to take steps to eliminate or control those risks.

The regulations apply to all substances which can have an adverse effect on health (except those with special hazards which are covered by their own regulations). These include:

- substances which are listed as toxic, very toxic, harmful, irritant or corrosive under the **Chemicals (Hazard, Information and Packaging for Supply) Regulations 1994**
- substances with maximum occupational exposure limits
- harmful micro-organisms
- substantial quantitites of dust
- carcinogens
- any substance not mentioned above but which creates a health hazard comparable to any of them.

The first step is for the employer to assess what risk (if any) is posed by substances used. This exercise must be carried out by a competent person. This can mean anything from a member of the management team in a small company using very few hazardous substances, to a whole team of specialists in a large chemical plant. Where appropriate, external consultants can be used. Whoever does the job will need to draw upon the knowledge and experience of managers in making their assessment. For example, before putting a report together, the assessor will probably need to tour around the workplace taking note of every hazardous substance that is used or produced, together with any problems which exist. The manager of one particular process might have noticed that there is a high level of sickness absence amongst his or her subordinates. Such information will be invaluable in assessing possible health risks. The assessor must also evaluate measures that are used to control exposure to substances, so managers may be asked to comment on how effective they feel existing procedures are and to suggest improvements. It is worth noting that where an employer has carried out an assessment under the **Control of Substances Hazardous to Health Regulations 1994**, there is no need to assess the same substances all over again in order to comply with the **Management of Health**

and Safety at Work Regulations 1992 (see page 8). Provided the assessment is regularly reviewed and remains valid, then duplication is unnecessary.

The next step under the **Control of Substances Hazardous to Health Regulations 1994** is to prevent or control exposure to hazardous substances. Prevention is the preferred option, and the employer should consider whether this can be achieved by, for example, substituting the harmful substance with a less harmful one. Where prevention is not possible, then exposure must be brought down to acceptable limits by suitable control measures, eg isolating the work process in some way. Again managers will be in a good position to make suggestions as to how this might be achieved. Generally speaking, the risk will be seen as adequately controlled provided that daily exposure to the substance at the level maintained is harmless to most people. However, for certain substances which are harmful to health if they are inhaled, there are specific exposure limits which must be observed. It is only where such control measures are inadequate that employers are allowed to resort to the use of personal protective equipment, eg face masks. Where such equipment is needed, however, both employers and employees have a duty to ensure that it is properly used and maintained. Employees must be sure to report any defects they discover to their employers at once. Obviously managers have a crucial role in stressing the importance of these matters to their subordinates and making sure that they do what is required of them.

A further requirement under the regulations is for exposure to hazardous substances to be monitored. This includes checking personal exposure (in some cases individual health checks will be appropriate), as well as checking that equipment used for controlling exposure is working properly.

However, even the most thorough arrangements will fail unless each individual employee is aware of the risks associated with their work and how those risks may be avoided. Managers must ensure, therefore, that their staff are properly instructed and trained in all these matters to ensure their own and everyone else's safety and well-being.

No member of the workforce should be set to work with potentially dangerous materials unless the manager is sure that adequate safety measures have been taken. Written procedures should be distributed to all employees; the manager should then check that procedures are being followed and monitor their effectiveness. Again, any queries or difficulties should be referred without delay to the person responsible for overall company safety.

CHIP Regulations

The **Chemicals (Hazard Information and Packaging for Supply) Regulations 1994** (as amended in 1996) specifically affect those who supply dangerous substances and/or preparations. However, all employers should be aware of these provisions so that they know the safety information they should have in relation to dangerous substances and/or preparations used at work.

The purpose of the regulations is to protect people and the environment from the ill-effects of substances and/or preparations. They place certain obligations on suppliers to:

- identify the hazards and risks of the substances and/or preparations they supply (and "classify" them — see below)
- give information about those hazards and risks to the people they supply substances and/or preparations to, and
- package the substances and/or preparations safely.

Similar requirements are placed on those who transport substances and/or preparations by road or rail.

Before supplying a dangerous substance or preparation, a supplier must classify it into one or more of the categories specified in the regulations (eg toxic, corrosive, explosive, flammable). The supply also has to provide the recipient with safety information about the substance or preparation by means of appropriate labelling and (where the substance or preparation is to be used in connection with work) a safety data sheet.

Protective Clothing and Equipment

There are detailed regulations requiring employers to supply and ensure the use of protective clothing in certain processes relating to asbestos, chemicals, glass, ionising radiation, foundries, lead, pottery, etc. (Furthermore, in these circumstances the employer may not charge for the clothing or equipment provided.) More generally, where employees are exposed to other hazardous substances, the provision of protective clothing may form part of the employer's strategy to comply with his duties under the **Control of Substances Hazardous to Health Regulations 1994** (see above).

However, there is a wider duty placed upon employers to provide protective clothing under the **Personal Protective Equipment at Work Regulations 1992**. These require that personal protective equipment (PPE) must be supplied and used at work wherever risks to health and safety cannot be adequately controlled by other means. In other words, PPE must be used as a last resort.

PPE is defined as any equipment which is designed to be worn or held by people at work to protect them from health and safety risks. This embraces an enormous variety of items such as safety helmets and boots, goggles and gloves, and clothing to protect against extreme temperatures, poor visibility and adverse weather conditions.

In order to ensure that employees are adequately protected, employers need to give careful consideration to what risks there are and what sort of equipment will provide suitable protection. Needless to say, identifying the risk is a crucial step in the process because unless this is done properly, then the PPE which is provided may prove useless.

When choosing PPE, a number of factors need to be taken into account. As well as being appropriate and effective for the task, it needs to fit the wearer comfortably and correctly, and so should be capable of being adjusted. Consideration should also be given to the conditions in which it is to be used, the nature of the job and the state of health of the wearer. Attention must be paid to individual needs. For example, there may be complaints that a safety shoe is unsuitable for the feet of a particular employee. Any such problems need to be investigated with reference to medical opinion and different but equally safe equipment found where necessary. Similar difficulties may arise in connection with other items of clothing, for example where an individual claims that he or she is allergic to a certain type of material. Again, referral to the experts should determine whether the complaint is genuine and, if so, what the solution may be.

When an employer makes it a condition of employment that workers use safety equipment or clothing, it is the employee's duty to comply with this. It follows, therefore, that if employees refuse to do so or repeatedly ignore these instructions, their conduct should lead to disciplinary action. Indeed, the employee may be open to prosecution under s.7 of the **Health and Safety at Work, etc Act 1974** for not making proper use of protective equipment or clothing provided. It will be negligent on the employer's part if no — or half-hearted — action is taken. It is necessarily the manager who will be in the front line in ensuring both that safety wear is used at all appropriate times and that prompt action is taken to deal appropriately with any resistance.

A note should be added regarding possible problems which may arise in connection with ethnic minority groups where particular safety or hygiene requirements may conflict with their religion and are therefore potentially discriminatory. Such cases should be referred to the personnel department who may wish to contact the Commission for Racial Equality if there is no obvious solution. Many difficulties can now be overcome. For example, beards may be covered by a snood in industries where they are normally prohibited for reasons of hygiene. In other instances, however, the problem may be more intractable. In one particular area, the law is quite specific. On construction sites, employers must provide employees with safety helmets and must ensure that they are worn whenever there is a risk of head injury. In practical terms this means that the person in charge of the site must draw up rules to say when and where hard hats should be worn and managers must make sure that those rules are observed. However, an employer cannot require a Sikh employee who is wearing a turban to wear a safety helmet on a construction site — the law provides a specific exemption to cover the situation. Where an employer feels that it is essential for the sake of employees' safety to introduce a "hard hats" rule in any other dangerous situation, and a Sikh employee feels unable to comply and claims racial discrimination, an employer will need to be able to demonstrate that the rule was completely justifiable.

One final practical point is to ensure that where several items of PPE are being used at the same time, they are compatible and do not render each other ineffective.

The Working Environment

Many aspects of the working environment affect employees' comfort and well-being during the working day. The **Workplace (Health, Safety and Welfare) Regulations 1992** lay down minimum requirements in relation to a number of matters, including:

- temperature
- ventilation
- lighting
- room size
- workstations and seating
- floors and traffic routes

- windows and ventilators
- doors and gates
- escalators
- toilets
- washing facilities
- drinking water
- rest rooms
- facilities for changing and storing clothes.

Some of the areas covered by the regulations are considered in detail below.

Temperature

From 1 January 1996, the **Workplace (Health, Safety and Welfare) Regulations 1992** — which already applied to new workplaces (ie those in use for the first time since 1 January 1993) — replaced previous provisions of the **Factories Act 1961** and the **Offices, Shops and Railway Premises Act 1963**. The 1992 regulations state that workroom temperatures in factories, offices, shops and other workplaces must be "reasonable" for the people employed. The Approved Code of Practice and guidance which accompanies the regulations says that 16°C is reasonable, although where work is strenuous and involves physical effort, this may be reduced to 13°C. No means of heating can be used which is likely to cause harmful fumes or other health and safety risks.

In circumstances where the employer is unable to achieve the minimum temperature in the workplace, it is reasonable to expect employees to hold themselves available for work, perhaps in the canteen, and to restart as soon as the temperature rises sufficiently. When a temporary lack of power causes a drop in temperature, employers should consider the use of independent forms of local heating, the supply of hot drinks to workers, provision of extra clothing, etc.

Similarly, in the case of a heatwave the employer's duty of care is to maintain a reasonable temperature in the circumstances. Cold drinks, fans and additional breaks may alleviate the situation.

Managers generally have little control over work temperature and probably the most important role they can play when it becomes a problem is that of communicator. What is needed from the workforce at times like these is co-operation. To achieve this the manager needs to be able to explain why the extreme of temperature has occurred and how the company is attempting to put matters right. Any constructive suggestions should be gratefully received. The more managers do to foster a spirit of co-operation among their subordinates, the more likely are employees to be helpful in this situation.

Lighting

Sufficient and suitable lighting (whether natural or artificial) must be provided in all parts of premises where people are working or passing through. Good housekeeping will ensure that faulty bulbs and strip lights are replaced and routinely maintained and that windows and lamps are cleaned regularly. However, *too much* light can also be a problem, causing glare which may result in impaired vision. Advice should be sought on ways of reducing glare when the obvious ways of re-siting machinery or using blinds are not possible. Particular machines, eg VDUs and woodworking machinery, have specific lighting requirements to ensure that the operator works in safety and relative comfort.

Managers need to be alert to the fact that inadequate or inappropriate lighting may be a cause of tiredness and stress amongst employees. Where the problem cannot be solved within the department it may be appropriate to suggest that an expert in lighting design be called in to recommend alterations.

The **Workplace (Health, Safety and Welfare) Regulations 1992** state that sufficient and suitable lighting must be provided. Wherever possible, natural light should be utilised and where it is, windows and skylights should be regularly cleaned. Where the employer relies upon artificial lighting and its failure could create a danger, then emergency lighting must be provided.

Ventilation

Under the **Health and Safety at Work, etc Act 1974**, employers have a general duty to ensure that work premises are ventilated in such a way as to ensure that no one's health and safety is put at risk. More specifically, from 1 January 1996 onwards all workplaces had to comply with the **Workplace (Health, Safety and Welfare) Regulations 1992**, which contain certain requirements in respect of ventilation.

The regulations distinguish between "comfort" ventilation and "extraction" ventilation. Comfort ventilation is concerned with providing fresh air throughout the workplace, whereas extraction ventilation is about removing harmful dust and fumes. The regulations state that all workplaces must be suitably and effectively ventilated with fresh or purified air. The accompanying code of practice states that in many cases sufficient ventilation can be achieved simply by opening windows. Where this is not enough, however, a system of mechanical ventilation must be used, and this should be provided with a failure warning device. As a guide, the fresh air rate should not fall below five to eight litres of fresh air per person per second. When assessing what is needed, account should be taken of factors such as the nature of the work being carried out, whether it is strenuous, and how closely people are working together.

In some situations, general ventilation will be inadequate for dealing with the harmful dust or fumes which are generated by the work process. In such cases, consideration will need to be given to an effective extraction system in order to comply with the variety of specific regulations which govern this area. These include regulations covering the construction industry, the control of asbestos and ionising radiations.

The human body needs an adequate supply of oxygen to function correctly and so correct ventilation is a very important aspect of the working environment.

Regular maintenance and monitoring should ensure that the ventilation system is functioning properly at all times. If, however, a manager is concerned about dust or fume levels, for example, it is essential that such anxiety be transmitted straightaway to the responsible member of management so that a check can be made.

A problem seems to be arising over centrally heated or air-conditioned offices where people are unable to open windows. Headaches, general malaise, tiredness and stress appear to be associated with this environment and the condition has been dubbed "sick building syndrome". If there appears to be a genuine problem in this regard, the company should consult experts on whether the current system provides a correct balance.

Smoking

However well ventilated a room may be, problems can still arise over cigarette or cigar smoke. Increasingly, smoking at work is regarded as unacceptable and many employers are introducing smoking bans (see page 61). In any event, under the **Workplace (Health, Safety and Welfare) Regulations 1992**, rest rooms and rest areas should include suitable arrangements to protect non-smokers from discomfort caused by tobacco smoke.

Requests for a smoking ban are likely to come to the line manager in the first instance. Careful consultation is needed with all staff, and if a total ban is decided upon then it should be introduced reasonably and with sufficient warning. Where possible, alternative arrangements should be made for smokers, eg provision of a room or area where smoking is allowed. Employees should be given adequate warning of the consequences of not complying, and should be clear about what disciplinary measures will be taken. Those who wish to give up smoking should be offered as much practical help and support as possible.

On the whole, it is prudent for employers to protect employees from passive smoking by introducing a total smoking ban in the workplace, as there is a strong likelihood of future litigation in this area.

Rest Rooms

All workers must be provided with suitable and easily accessible rest facilities. They must include appropriate arrangements to protect non-smokers from discomfort caused by tobacco smoke. Suitable rest facilities must be provided for pregnant women and women who are breastfeeding.

Where workers regularly eat meals in the workplace or where food eaten in the workplace is likely to become contaminated, suitable and sufficient facilities for eating meals must be provided. Work seats in offices or other clean environments may be acceptable as rest facilities so long as staff are not unduly disturbed during their rest periods. There should be hot drinks facilities, and if hot food cannot be readily obtained, then workers may need to be provided with the means to heat their own food. Canteens may be used as rest facilities, provided workers are not obliged to buy food.

8 Fair Dismissal

Employees with at least two years' continuous service have the right not to be unfairly dismissed.

Dismissals can be fair only if the reason is capability, conduct, redundancy, avoiding breach of the law or another substantial reason justifying dismissal. In the context of health and safety it is possible for dismissals to be necessary on grounds of either: capability — an employee's mental or physical state making performance of the job difficult, dangerous or impossible; conduct — employees flouting rules or procedures on health and safety; or to avoid breaking the law.

Reviewed in this chapter is the procedure which should be followed before employees are dismissed for any of these reasons.

Capability Dismissals

Capability dismissal covers a wide range of performance problems. It can be "fair" to dismiss people if they can no longer cope, for *whatever* reason. Dismissal by reason of capability may be caused by a person becoming so ill that they are unable to work for a long period, or their health will suffer if they continue to work, or their state of health will make it dangerous for them to continue to do the job. The procedure for each differs slightly.

Inability

If employees are simply unable to do the job and, as a result, may be a health or safety hazard to themselves or to other employees, this could obviously be a fair reason for dismissal. However, there are three important factors which must be borne in mind:

- a previously good worker who suddenly appears to be incapable may well have a health problem and a thorough investigation will be necessary
- if the incapability is due to lack of training, the dismissal may well be unfair
- dismissal should only be considered if further training does not help and there is no alternative work which the employee could be offered.

Ill-health Absences

Employees who are away from work on long-term sickness absence may be fairly dismissed but a reasonable procedure must be followed. Essentially the employees must be consulted, permission requested to approach their doctor, in accordance with the **Access to Medical Reports Act 1988** or **Access to Health Records Act 1990**, the doctor's opinion sought as to the likely length of the absence, and a decision then made as to whether the job can be held open.

Other Ill-health Problems

There are many other aspects of ill-health which can cause health and safety problems.

Returning

Employees who have been away on long-term sick leave might try to return to work before they are fit, perhaps because they are worried about losing their jobs. In such cases it would not be unreasonable to require a note from their doctor confirming that they are fit to resume work. To allow employees to return to work before they are fit — and having reason to believe they are not fit — could constitute a breach of the employer's general duty of care for employees' health, safety and welfare.

Working but unfit

It may be the case that employees continue to work but their physical or mental state makes this difficult or dangerous. Examples might be an ageing employee doing a strenuous job and finding it more and more difficult, an employee who is verging on a nervous breakdown operating dangerous machinery, or an employee engaged in food handling who is suffering from an infection. It is important to note, however, that the **Disability Discrimination Act 1995** requires the employer to adapt workplaces or work procedures, where reasonably practicable, when an employee develops or has a disability which does not affect his or her fundamental ability to do a job.

The best procedure to follow in such cases is to discuss the problem with the employees concerned, seek their agreement to undergo a medical examination and then suspend them on full pay pending notification from their doctor concerning their fitness for work. Should they be deemed unfit, the normal sick leave provisions should apply. In such cases it is important that the doctor is given details of the type of work the people are employed to do and is notified of any special factors which apply to their job, eg whether they have to drive, lift heavy weights or operate machinery, etc.

An employee who refuses to undergo a medical examination may be fairly dismissed (provided a fair procedure is followed), if the company decides that continued employment will pose a significant risk. The key aspects of such a procedure are that the employer should consider whether transfer to other work might resolve the problem, discuss the matter fully with the employee and, where transfer is not feasible, warn that continued refusal to undergo a medical examination will result in dismissal. At this stage it would be best to suspend the employee on full pay for a few days to give time for thought.

Continued work poses risks

There are certain industrial injuries and diseases which, if not treated in time, may prove to be disabling. One example is tenosynovitis which constitutes a significant hazard for people whose occupation involves constant repetition of finger and thumb movements (see page 56). If it is not diagnosed and dealt with at an early stage, the problem may grow worse and become irreversible, such that even a change of occupation will not help. If a manager is alerted to any health problem which may be due to an employee's job, it must be investigated. If it transpires that it *is* linked to the person's occupation, early action must be taken. This might be in the form of protective equipment, of modifications to the job or the environment or, if neither of these would be effective or practicable, consideration would have to be given to transferring the employee to alternative work. Only if this was not possible would dismissal be fair. Extra care should be taken in dealing with this situation because a person who has developed tenosynovitis would also be covered under the provisions of the **Disability Discrimination Act 1995**.

Failure to take these steps could result in the company being prosecuted under the **Health and Safety at Work, etc Act 1974** and would enable the employee to make a claim for damages in respect of the injury suffered.

Misconduct

Dismissals for misconduct normally fit into one of two categories — misconduct which, after due warnings, will result in dismissal, or gross misconduct which is so serious that the employee is dismissed for a first breach of the rules. In either case, for the dismissal to be fair, the employer must carry out a thorough investigation and follow a fair procedure.

Fair Procedure

There is a code of practice on discipline which is produced by the Advisory, Conciliation and Arbitration Service (ACAS) and sets out helpful guidelines on the procedure which should be followed before an employee is dismissed on conduct grounds. The code states that the essential points of the disciplinary procedure are as follows:

- the procedure should be in writing
- disciplinary matters should be dealt with quickly
- the disciplinary sanctions should be indicated
- the levels of management with authority to take disciplinary action should be specified but, in general, employees' immediate superiors should not have the power to dismiss them without reference to more senior management
- employees should be given details of complaints against them and have the right to state their case before disciplinary decisions are made — at this meeting they should have the right to be accompanied by a trade union representative or colleague of their choice
- other than in exceptional cases (see below) employees should not be dismissed for a first offence
- no disciplinary action should be taken until a careful investigation has been undertaken — even if an employee appears to have been caught red-handed there may be an explanation
- employees should have the right to appeal against disciplinary decisions.

Giving Warnings

The ACAS code recommends the following sequence of warnings:

- in the case of minor offences the individual should be given a formal oral warning, and in more serious cases, a first written warning

- further misconduct might warrant a final written warning.

In either case it is important that the warning spells out the nature of the offence and the likely consequences of further offences.

Safety Rules

It is important that employees are aware of actions which will result in disciplinary steps being taken. It might seem obvious that any fooling around near machinery is unacceptable, but newcomers to the industry may not appreciate the hazards. While it is not possible to list every action which will be treated as misconduct, disciplinary rules should pay due regard to health and safety and should also spell out the types of action which will be treated as gross misconduct or, in the absence of mitigating factors, result in summary dismissal. For instance, smoking in an area containing highly flammable substances will usually be treated as gross misconduct, while smoking in areas which have been declared to be no-smoking zones, perhaps because of the wishes of employees, will normally result in a warning being given.

Dismissal Without Prior Warnings

Dismissal for a first offence may be warranted in cases of gross misconduct — behaviour which is such that no reasonable employer could be expected to tolerate the continued employment of that person. Such conduct will, of course, vary from organisation to organisation. The important point is that the employees concerned should realise that their behaviour will lead to dismissal. However, as always, employees should not be dismissed until there has been a thorough investigation and the complaint has been put to the employee, giving him or her a reasonable opportunity to defend their actions or put forward any mitigating factors.

Dismissal might also be warranted for a first breach of the rules or procedure because of the seriousness of the *consequences* rather than the conduct itself. In the case of an airline pilot, for example, one single lapse could have extremely serious consequences. If an employee operating dangerous machinery failed to follow proper safety procedures, so that serious danger to life and limb could have ensued, dismissal might be appropriate if the employer had reason to believe that the offence might be repeated. Indeed, if serious action was not taken and the employee repeated the behaviour, injuring another employee as a result, the employer would probably be found liable for the injury and have to pay substantial compensation.

Dismissal to Avoid Breach of the Law

There will be occasions when dismissal is warranted through no fault at all of the employee. If it is impossible for the employee to continue to work without involving either employee or employer in breaking the law, dismissal will be fair if no alternative work is available. For example, if an HGV driver loses his or her licence as a result of the onset of a disability which is likely to be long-term, continuing to work as a driver is clearly not an option.

Under the regulations covering those who work with ionising radiation, indiarubber and other hazardous substances, employees must cease working if their health is being put at risk. Where no alternative work is available and a worker is suspended, payment must be made at the normal rate for up to 26 weeks (see also pages 73 and 74). Employers would clearly need to consider dismissal if there was a continuing and prolonged problem.

Constructive Dismissal

"Constructive" dismissal occurs when an employer acts in breach of an employee's contract and the employee leaves as a direct result. In law this is treated as a dismissal and the employee may make an unfair dismissal complaint.

Since employers have a duty to take reasonable care of their employees' health, safety and welfare, it follows that this will be an implied term of employees' contracts. In the context of this book, health or safety grievances which are not investigated could entitle the employee to leave and make a successful constructive dismissal claim.

Any complaint should be investigated thoroughly, however trivial it may seem at first hearing, and where appropriate, in conjunction with a safety officer and safety representative. Where it is found after investigation that the complaint has no validity, the manager should reassure the employee by giving a clear explanation of how that conclusion was arrived at. It may emerge that in fact the employee has other concerns and the particular complaint was a symptom of a more general dissatisfaction which needs to be dealt with.

When the complaint does appear to have some substance, remedial action needs to be taken. An example is in the case of an employee who is required to wear safety goggles over glasses. The glasses mist up and there is a problem with light reflection. A complaint to management goes unheeded and the employee is therefore left in the position of either risking eye injury by not using the goggles or terminating the employment. In such a case the employer will not have acted reasonably in dealing with a safety complaint and the employee is likely to succeed in a constructive unfair dismissal claim.

Similar considerations apply to health matters; for example, an employee may be transferred to an area of the operation where materials are used to which he or she is allergic.

To sum up, the golden rule for managers is *never* dismiss a complaint out of hand. Always look into it carefully and see that appropriate action is taken as soon as possible.

Health and Safety Employment Protection

Since 1993, employees have been protected against being dismissed or being put at any other disadvantage for carrying out (or proposing to carry out) certain actions relating to health and safety. These provisions formed part of the **Trade Union Reform and Employment Rights Act 1993** and are now contained in the **Employment Rights Act 1996**. Protection is extended to all workers regardless of their hours of work, age or length of service. It is automatically unfair to dismiss employees who:

- are performing health and safety responsibilities designated by their employer
- have left a dangerous part of the workplace if there is believed to be some serious or imminent danger which could not be averted, and are refusing to return whilst the danger persists
- are bringing a reasonable health and safety concern to the employer's attention in the absence of a representative or relevant committee
- are performing functions as employer-acknowledged health and safety representatives or committee members
- are taking appropriate steps to protect themselves or others in circumstances of serious or imminent danger.

In the last category, whether or not the steps taken were appropriate will be judged by reference to all the circumstances at the time. It may be possible for the employer to show that the steps taken were so negligent that dismissal was a reasonable response.

Where an employee wishes to bring a claim under these provisions, the matter goes before an industrial tribunal, and compensation may be awarded if the complaint is well founded.

9 Increasing Employee Awareness

It has been stressed how important it is to make employees aware of the many safety hazards present in the workplace in order to ensure a safe system of work. The manager should ensure that employees always keep safety at the forefront of their minds. Staff must be ready to act quickly if an accident does happen. They should also consider whether anything they do is likely to increase the risk of an accident. Employees must be aware of the company safety rules and be quite clear that these must be obeyed. Safety awareness should be a natural part of the working day. People frequently learn by example and good or bad habits can spread quickly around the workplace. If the manager starts by making existing employees safety conscious, this will spread to new recruits, temporary workers, etc. The aim is prevention rather than cure. Managers need to be extremely vigilant and observant when it comes to safety, both in and out of their own departments. They need to consider carefully the potential hazards and dangers, and make sure that these do not happen.

Creating and Maintaining a Safe Environment

Primarily the manager needs to have a clear idea of what needs to be done to create and maintain a safe workplace.

Risk Assessment

An effective way to identify problems is through risk assessment (see pages 8 and 10). Under the **Management of Health and Safety at Work Regulations 1992**, all employers are required to carry out an assessment of health and safety risks arising from their work activities. In addition, a number of other sets of regulations covering, for example, noise, display screen equipment and hazardous substances, contain specific requirements in relation to risk assessment. In essence, risk assessment involves considering what, at work, can cause harm to people, so that sufficient precautions can be taken.

Safety Audits

As well as risk assessment, many companies carry out regular safety audits to pinpoint the company's safety strengths and weaknesses. Basically, safety audits are surveys which identify all the separate parts of a job which affect safety, eg:

- mechanical processes
- chemical processes
- electrical processes
- employee attitudes
- management policy
- "housekeeping"
- safety equipment
- training
- emergency procedures
- individual protection requirements
- environmental factors.

Under each part (or heading) a number of questions are asked of a particular job, as shown below.

Housekeeping

1. Is electrical equipment unplugged and put away when it is no longer being used?
2. Are all spillages cleaned up straightaway?
3. Are there any trailing wires which people could trip over?

Training

1. Do new employees have the relevant company safety rules explained to them on their first day?
2. Are contractors and agency employees trained in safety?
3. Are records kept of training given?

Employee attitudes

1. Do employees take training seriously?
2. Which takes priority for employees — speed or safety?
3. Do employees report any situations they think a safety risk?

These questions are normally drawn up by the safety officer. Managers with their wealth of experience can offer an important contribution by making sure that all the relevant questions are asked. Only they will know some of the less obvious safety hazards.

A safety audit should be approached with the same seriousness and attention to detail as a post-accident investigation. It should be remembered that the aim of the audit is prevention rather than cure, through identifying and eliminating actual and potential safety hazards. Reference should be made to accident reports, safety committee findings, in-house specialists and, most importantly, the person actually doing the job.

Safety Inspections

If a full safety audit is not practicable, managers can simply make sure that the whole of their area is regularly checked, at least once a week. (Those working in high-risk workplaces should make more frequent checks.)

It is a good idea to have an inspection checklist of all areas drawn up, including every item that needs to be checked.

The checklist should ask such questions as:

- Are aisles and gangways clear?
- Is noise at a level where instructions or the fire bell can be clearly heard?

- Is necessary safety equipment available and used?
- Are all dangerous machine parts properly guarded?
- Is stored material checked for dates?
- Is racking and shelving overloaded or stacked too high?
- Are safety rules being followed?

Regular inspections and audits are one way of making employees aware that the manager is committed to safety. Spot checks are also a good idea if a manager feels that certain employees are not being consistent and only following safety rules on Monday morning (or whenever the inspection takes place).

In many organisations managers will carry out the safety audit themselves on a regular basis, eg once a week. This should ensure that problems are dealt with straightaway or as soon as is practicably possible. The manager can then draw up a list of all the problems revealed by the audit, such as overcrowded storage areas, unused eye protection, unstable shelving, etc.

Managers will often need to pass on their findings to higher management, in writing, wherever possible. Reports may include recommendations for changes to company safety rules or notification of machinery malfunctions.

Many problem areas can be improved simply by the manager thinking through ways to make them more safe.

Safety audits are useful tools for measuring and monitoring health and safety performance, and confirming (or otherwise) the effectiveness of the control measures determined by risk assessment.

Training

Safety training is an area that is important, yet is frequently neglected. If approached in the right way it need not take up too much time and money, and can even be fun. It should be done on a proactive rather than a reactive basis, that is, taking preventive measures rather than just "fire-fighting" or reacting to a crisis.

Safety training needs to be approached systematically. If it is done in a haphazard fashion some employees will miss out and their lack of training could cause accidents. The simplest way to avoid this is to draw up a form for each employee listing all safety training given and, most importantly, the date on which it took place. This can be kept on the employee's file and inspected regularly, ensuring that when a manager moves to another department or leaves the company, his or her replacement can quickly see what has been done in the past.

Legal Requirements

The principal legal requirements were reviewed in the introduction to this book and, in particular, mention was made of the **Health and Safety at Work, etc Act 1974**, which imposes a general duty on every employer to provide the necessary training to ensure the health and safety at work of all employees, so far as is reasonably practicable. The general duty to train will include providing:

- induction training programmes for all new recruits
- regular refresher training for all employees
- training for employees who are transferred or promoted, before the new job is started.

When looking at training the employer should pay attention to employees' individual needs. Training provisions should be set out in the company safety policy statement (see page 35).

In addition, the requirement to train is explicitly referred to in the **Management of Health and Safety at Work Regulations 1992**, and in the regulations which govern the use of DSE, work equipment and protective clothing.

Dangerous Processes

There are specific regulations covering training where certain dangerous processes are involved, such as the use of abrasive wheels, power presses and woodworking machines. (For further information see *Croner's Health and Safety at Work.*)

Young People

Under the **Health and Safety (Young Persons) Regulations 1997**, which came into effect on 3 March 1997, certain obligations are laid on employers in relation to the employment of young persons. These include specific risk assessment for the safety of young persons and specific requirements in relation to the provision of information to young persons and their guardians. Certain types of work are also prohibited for young persons, except in certain circumstances. These types of work are:

- work which is beyond his or her physical or psychological capacity
- work which involves exposure to carcinogens, toxic substances, teratogins or substances causing heritable damage
- work which involves exposure to radiation
- work which involves a risk of accidents which a young person could not have recognised or avoided due to lack of experience or training
- work which involves extremes of cold or heat
- work which involves noise, or
- work which involves vibration.

Young persons may undertake such work (provided they are not aged below 16) if:

- it is necessary to their training
- they are supervised by a competent person, and

- any risk is reduced to the lowest level that is reasonably practicable.

Full details are given in *Croner's Health and Safety at Work* and *Croner's Reference Book for Employers*. Youth Training trainees are included as employees for the purposes of the **Health and Safety at Work, etc Act 1974**, and they are thus given the same protection as other members of the workforce.

Identifying Training Needs

The first step to be taken is to identify the training that needs to take place by drawing up a list of what employees need to know and comparing this with what they actually do know. In considering what training needs exist, the following are useful sources.

Safety Audits and Inspections

These will reveal many training needs (see page 30).

Accident and Safety Committee Reports

These serve to highlight proven problem areas and safety training needs.

The Job

One of the main ways of identifying training needs is by looking at the job itself. A good starting point is the job description, where one is available. The manager should pick out the key tasks of the job and the standards expected. Some job training needs will be fairly obvious, such as a machine operator needing to be trained in the correct method of operation.

Those people who need to use safety equipment must be trained how to use it correctly and told what to do if it is not working properly.

The manager should try to think through the job and all the processes it entails from start to finish. For managers who are making a first attempt to identify job-related training needs, it should be realised that this is an ongoing process. Nobody will be able to identify all problem areas at one attempt; it is necessary to keep eyes and ears open for as yet unidentified areas, consulting with employees as much as possible.

The Environment

All working environments possess safety hazards, some more apparent than others.

High Risk Areas

Many managers work in areas of known high risk, such as work involving the handling of hazardous substances (see page 108). There are specific regulations and requirements to be observed in certain industries and further details can be found in *Croner's Health and Safety at Work*. Thorough training about the dangers involved and precautionary measures that must be taken is of crucial importance in such work situations.

The manager's job here is to make sure that the existing training is adequate. Both employees and managers must make sure that this is so. Any doubts should be brought to the attention of the manager responsible.

For example, are all areas covered? Does retraining occur? Are people who do not work in, but simply pass through, such areas properly informed? If managers are to identify training needs in high-risk (or indeed low-risk) areas, it is essential to know exactly what the risk is in order to give adequate and accurate training.

If the work involves contact with one of the many chemical substances used at the workplace it is essential to know exactly what harmful or dangerous effects it has. If this is not clear from the packaging, managers should ask their safety officer or senior manager to clarify the issue with the manufacturer or supplier by requesting the appropriate safety data sheet.

Employees Who Travel

Employees whose jobs involve travelling away from site will be subject to hazards that are out of the manager's sight and thus possibly out of mind. When considering training needs for such employees, managers should look first to the obvious hazards, for example those involved in driving. It is possible to draw up a list of such hazards, for instance risks whilst driving increase when:

- weather conditions are poor
- mechanical faults go unnoticed or unchecked
- the driver is tired, or under the influence of drink or drugs
- the driver is in too much of a hurry.

Thus some training needs are quite clear whilst others will only be identified by the person actually doing the job. Such employees can sometimes feel out on a limb. Increasing the overall awareness of the workforce will help to counteract this. Managers should also encourage those who drive to talk about any particular safety problems they face and try to work out preventive measures and solutions together. It is very important for managers to let such employees know that they are concerned about employee safety both in and away from the main site.

Isolated Employees

Special consideration needs to be given to staff who are required to work on their own for some or all of the time. Managers should make quite sure that such employees are crystal clear about all safety procedures. If a fire breaks out, for example, these employees will have no one to ask or to remind them what they should and should not do. They should be visited or rung regularly by colleagues to check that everything is all right. The manager should also ensure that building security is adequate and that the employee can contact people quickly should a problem arise.

Some employees, such as shop assistants, may be at extra personal risk by working on their own when handling money. This makes them vulnerable to potentially violent crimes. Every attempt should be made to minimise the risk by taking measures such as frequent emptying of tills, the installation of video cameras and well-publicised alarms, etc. Such employees must be told clearly what to do if someone acts in a threatening manner towards them.

Common Problems

Slipping and tripping accidents and problems due to incorrect lifting techniques can occur in all working environments. They make up nearly 50% of all office accidents. A simple slip, for example, can easily cause a broken ankle. This will give the employee considerable discomfort and may require up to two months or more off work. In some cases what appears to be a relatively straightforward slip or trip can cause permanent disability.

Measures to prevent such accidents should be included in the company safety policy and rules. Whilst looking at the training needs in this area, the manager may discover risks which should be reported to and dealt with by senior management. These matters are covered on page 85.

Managers should make employees aware of the risks they run in disobeying company safety rules or in acting thoughtlessly. To many employees the "risk" of not following safety procedures is of being reprimanded and, at worst, disciplined. It must be made quite clear that the actual risks range from a person having to take time off work, often with less than full pay, to permanent disability or death in some cases. The aim of all managers is to make employees wise before rather than after the event.

Problem Areas

In identifying what employees need to know about safety, the manager must first establish what individual employees already know. Certain employees will have greater needs or take longer to become safety conscious than others. Different employees have different attitudes towards safety. Employees needing special attention include the following.

New Recruits

It is often wisest for managers to assume that new employees, whatever their qualifications or status, know nothing or very little about safety. This is so even when employees have come from organisations well known for high safety standards. The previous employers might have had different safety procedures and the employees will often be in need of some refresher training. The manager will need to assess how much training new employees need before they can start work, whether supervised or unsupervised.

Young People

In general, young people need a higher degree of training to take into account their inexperience and possible immaturity. Managers should anticipate a degree of irresponsibility among some young employees. They are generally more impressionable and, if unchecked, may follow bad examples rather than good ones. Employers are also required by the **Health and Safety (Young Persons) Regulations 1997** to provide information to young employees on how to undertake their duties in a safe manner.

Subcontractors

Managers must make sure that all subcontracted and agency emploees are given safety training and are safety conscious. Regular contractors should be vetted for safety performance. Such people may be hired on the understanding that they are fully trained; unfortunately most managers know from experience that this is not always the case. Such workers must be informed of all relevant safety provisions before they start work.

Language Difficulties

Some employees will have language difficulties, perhaps including poor reading and writing skills. Managers will often have to identify this problem themselves, as such people may be embarrassed to admit that they cannot read or write properly. It should be remembered that these employees may not be able to read safety notices. Managers should therefore take care to explain all procedures orally. Employees who do not speak English will need to have safety training and instructions translated.

Taking Action

Having identified the training needs, managers will find it useful to draw up an action plan. The three broad areas to be considered and tackled are:

- improvements to existing training
- new training needed
- maintaining safety awareness amongst employees.

Existing and New Training Methods

Where managers think that existing training is insufficient, they should point out the weak areas to senior management. In particular induction training, refresher training and training for transferred or promoted employees require careful consideration, and individual employees' needs must always be kept in mind. For example, certain groups of employees, such as those with language difficulties, may not be properly catered for. Findings from safety audits and inspections should be used to back up suggested changes in training. The best approach is to put forward positive ideas and suggestions to improve the company's current training, along with suggestions for different types of training.

Some managers hold weekly half-hour safety talks. These can work very well. The manager uses the time to talk about a particular problem area or to refresh employees' memories. If any accidents or near misses have occurred, these can be discussed, together with ways to make sure that they do not happen again. At these sessions employees should be encouraged to put forward any ideas they have to improve safety. Employees are thus being reminded regularly of the importance of safety.

Maintaining Safety Awareness

Probably the most important factor affecting employees' safety awareness is the manager's attitude. If a manager does not take safety seriously how can employees be expected to? Managers must draw the line quite clearly when employees' behaviour increases safety risks. It is quite clear that in high-risk workplaces, such as factories, fooling around will endanger employees. This is an area where the manager must be quite firm and should clearly state why such behaviour is inappropriate.

The manager should always be on the look out for safety risks or breaches of safety procedure. Anything amiss, however slight, should be pointed out straightaway. This should not stop when managers leave their own departments. If the manager notices something in the canteen, for example, he or she should make a point of reporting it to the relevant person immediately and letting employees know that this is being done. The message that safety comes first must be made very clear.

In-house company magazines and newsletters can be very useful in keeping employees aware of hazards. Some companies make use of cartoons. Methods like this attract people's attention and are particularly useful where language difficulties exist.

The key to safety-consciousness is constant evaluation. If standards in a certain area appear to be slipping, the manager must find out why. Perhaps some refresher training is needed, or the job itself may be partly to blame. Some disciplinary action may also be necessary (see page 124).

Production-related bonus schemes can also encourage standards to slip. If by not using a safety guard an employee saves time and earns more money, safety may be neglected. Where this is the case, the manager should pass this information on to senior management, who must find a solution. Some companies provide bonuses for departments or sites with a clear safety record. Where these are in operation, the manager must make sure that staff are not simply covering up accidents in order to get the bonus.

All safety incentive schemes should be well publicised. Some companies have arrangements where certificates or awards are given to departments or sites with good safety records. These can be a good way of making safety a high profile area.

Staff should always be encouraged to come forward with ideas on improving safety. Some companies have staff suggestion schemes, with cash or gifts as prizes for particularly useful suggestions. If employees have any form of performance appraisal or review, the manager should always make sure that the subject of safety comes up, praising those who are safety-conscious and picking up those who are not.

Appendix: Health and Safety Executive Addresses

An office of the Health and Safety Executive will share its address and telephone number with the Employment Medical Advisory Service for that area. These are listed below.

Head Offices

Rose Court, 2 Southwark Bridge, London SE1 9HF. Tel: 0171-717 6000.

Magdalen House, Trinity Road, Bootle, Merseyside L20 3QZ. Tel: 0151-951 4000.

1	**South West**	Inter City House Mitchell Lane Bristol BS1 6AN Tel: 0117-988 6000 Fax: 0117-926 2998	Avon, Cornwall, Devon, Gloucestershire, Somerset, Isles of Scilly
2	**South**	Priestley House Priestley Road Basingstoke RG24 9NW Tel: 01256 404000 Fax: 01256 404100	Berkshire, Dorset, Hampshire, Isle of Wight, Wiltshire
3	**South East**	3 East Grinstead House London Road East Grinstead RH19 lRR Tel: 01342 334200 Fax: 01342 334422	Kent, Surrey, East Sussex, West Sussex

4	**London NW**	Now merged with Area 5	
5	**London N**	Maritime House 1 Linton Road Barking IG11 8HF Tel: 0181-225 8000 Fax: 0181-235 8001 Chancel House Neasden Lane London NW10 2UD Tel: 0181-459 8855 Fax: 0181-459 2131	(Two offices covering the same boroughs) Barking and Dagenham, Barnet, Brent, Camden, Ealing, Enfield, Hackney, Haringey, Harrow, Havering, Islington, Newham, Redbridge, Tower Hamlets, Waltham Forest
6	**London S**	1 Long Lane London SE1 4PG Tel: 0171-556 2100 Fax: 0171-556 2200	Bexley, Bromley, City of London, Croydon, Greenwich, Hammersmith and Fulham, Hillingdon, Hounslow, Kensington and Chelsea, Kingston upon Thames, Lambeth, Lewisham, Merton, Richmond upon Thames, Southwark, Sutton Wandsworth, Westminster
7	**East Anglia**	39 Baddow Road Chelmsford Essex CM2 0HL Tel: 01245 706200 Fax: 01245 706222	Essex (except parts of the county covered by Area 5), Norfolk, Suffolk
8	**Northern Home Counties**	14 Cardiff Road Luton LUl lPP Tel: 01582 444200 Fax: 01582 444320	Bedfordshire, Buckinghamshire, Cambridgeshire, Hertfordshire

9	**East Midlands**	Belgrave House 1 Greyfriars Northampton NN1 2BS Tel: 01604 738300 Fax: 01604 738333	Leicestershire, Northamptonshire, Oxfordshire, Warwickshire
10	**West Midlands**	McLaren Building 2 Masshouse Circus Queensway Birmingham B4 7NP Tel: 0121-607 6200	
11	**Wales**	Brunel House 2 Fitzalan Road Cardiff CF2 lSH Tel: 01222 47377	Clwyd, Dyfed, Gwent, Gwynedd, Mid Glamorgan, Powys, South Glamorgan, West Glamorgan
12	**Marches**	Marches House Midway Newcastle-under-Lyme Staffordshire ST5 lDT Tel: 01782 602300 Fax: 01782 602400	Hereford and Worcester, Shropshire, Staffordshire
13	**North Midlands**	Pearson Building 55 Upper Parliament Street Nottingham NG1 6AU Tel: 0115-971 2800 Fax: 0115-971 2802	Derbyshire, Lincolnshire, Nottinghamshire
14	**South Yorkshire**	Sovereign House 110 Queens Street Sheffield Sl 2ES Tel: 0114-291 3000 Fax: 0114-291 2379	Humberside, South Yorkshire

15	**West and North Yorkshire**	8 St Paul's Street Leeds LSl 2LE Tel: 0113-283 4200 Fax: 0113-283 4296	North Yorkshire, West Yorkshire
16	**Greater Manches-ter**	Quay House Quay Street Manchester M3 3JB Tel: 0161-952 8200 Fax: 0161-952 8222	Greater Manchester
17	**Mersey-side**	The Triad Stanley Road Bootle L20 3PG Tel: 0151-479 2200 Fax: 0151-470 2201	Cheshire, Merseyside
18	**North West**	Victoria House Ormskirk Road Preston PRl lHH Tel: 01772 836200 Fax: 01772 836222	Cumbria, Lancashire
19	**North East**	Arden House Regent Centre Regent Farm Road Gosforth Newcastle-upon-Tyne NE3 3JN Tel: 0191-202 6200 Fax: 0191-202 6300	Cleveland, Durham, Northumberland, Tyne and Wear
20	**Scotland East**	Belford House 59 Belford Road Edinburgh EH4 3UE Tel: 0131-247 2000 Fax: 0131-247 2121	Borders, Central Fife, Grampian, Highland, Lothian, Tayside, island areas of Orkney and Shetland
21	**Scotland West**	West George Street Glasgow G2 4LW Tel: 0141-275 3000 Fax: 0141-275 3100	Dumfries and Galloway, Strathclyde, Western Isles

Further Information

Could you use Additional Copies of this Book?

Croner's Guide to Health and Safety is a pocket book designed for practical use by all those with management responsibilities. If you are a subscriber to *Croner's Reference Book for Employers* then this is one of a series of books on key areas of employment.

Are there other managers in your organisation who would benefit from having a copy to hand? If so, why not give them a copy to help them consolidate their knowledge and put into practice what they have learnt?

Additional copies at a special price of £9 plus £1.50 p&p per copy may be ordered by telephoning our Customer Services team on 0181-547 3333, quoting reference WFCV.

Conferences and Training

Attending a seminar is one of the best ways of keeping up with rapidly changing legislation, trends and new ideas. Croner Conferences and Training has many years' experience of running an extensive range of courses, all led by authoritative and experienced speakers. Courses are regularly offered on the following subjects:

Changing Contracts of Employment
The Effective Personnel Assistant
Essential Employment Law
The Effective Personnel Officer
Sensitive Issues at Work
The Lawful Termination of Employment
Transfer of Undertakings (Protection of Employment) Regulations
Investors in People

Disability Discrimination
Recruitment and Motivation
Employment Law Update
European Legislation
For further information on any of these courses please contact Conferences and Training on 0181-247 1251 or e-mail: training@croner.co.uk.

Croner In-Company Training

Courses offered on:
Employment Law
Management Skills
Health and Safety
Dangerous Substances
Importing/Exporting
VAT and Finance
and many more tailored to your needs, for all levels of staff, anywhere in Europe.

Our package comprises:

- a participative, tailored course
- a no obligation preliminary meeting
- full back-up documentation
- experienced and practical trainers
- a competitive price, estimated in advance
- backed by the Croner reputation.

For details of value for money, affordable courses for four or more staff, tailored to your needs, please contact Claire Spraggs on 0181-247 1243 or e-mail: training@croner.co.uk.

Croner Information Services

The current range of our information packages includes the following.

Croner's Reference Book for Employers

Known as the "Personnel Manager's Bible", this service covers all the legal obligations you face as an employer, in clear, precise, jargon-free language.

Contents Include

Health and Safety
Manpower
Pay
Employment Protection
Social Security
Pensions.

The Information Service Includes

- A loose-leaf reference guide
- Monthly updates to the loose-leaf
- Electronic disk version of the loose-leaf
- Fortnightly Employer's Briefing
- Series of pocketbooks.

Croner's Employment Law

An authoritative and comprehensive reference service covering the complex area of employment law, keeping you abreast of all the legislative changes, developments in courts and the European law, affecting the rights of individual employees.

Contents Include

Contracts
Discrimination
During Employment
Termination
Tribunal Procedures.

The Information Service Includes

- Two volume loose-leaf reference guide
- Monthly bulletins
- Monthly Questions and Answers
- Employment and Practice CD-ROM.

Croner's Personnel in Practice

A detailed reference source of tried and tested practical forms and procedures together with the UK's leading employment newsletter.

Contents Include

Introduction
Recruitment and Selection During Employment
General Employment Matters
Contracts
Termination.

The Information Service Includes

- A loose-leaf reference guide
- Quarterly updates to the loose-leaf
- Electronic disk version of the loose-leaf
- Fortnightly Employment Digest
- Monthly Employment Case Digest.

Croner's Pay and Benefits Sourcebook

Essential reading for anyone involved in designing salary packages and pay policy in a company.

Contents Include

Information Sources Pay
Working Time and Holidays
Benefits
Pay Bargaining.

The Information Service Includes

- A loose-leaf reference guide
- Quarterly updates to the loose-leaf
- Fortnightly Pay and Benefits Briefing
- Regular Special Reports.

Croner's Personnel Assistant's Handbook

Covering all the main areas of personnel including interviewing and report writing skills, employment law contracts, recruitment and selection, health and safety and much else. It is also an essential study guide for the Certificate in Personnel Practice course.

Contents Include

Basic Employment Law
Health and Safety
Recruitment and Selection
Induction
Conduct and Discipline
Absence
Salaries, Wages and Benefits
Termination of Employment
Letters — The Personal Touch.

The Information Service Includes

- A loose-leaf reference guide
- Quarterly updates to the loose-leaf
- Monthly bulletins
- Electronic disk version of the loose-leaf.

Croner's Team Leader's Briefing

A fortnightly newsletter containing articles and advice on the regular problems and issues which the team leader or supervisor faces.

Topics Covered Include

Recruitment and Selection
Disciplining Employees
Appraisal Interviewing
Leadership Skills
Team Building
Staff Training.

Contents of Each Issue Include

What's New?
A regular round-up of the latest news on employment, pay, benefits and health and safety issues.

The Team Leader's Role
Each issue takes a closer look at a particular area of responsibility of a team leader's job.

Specific issues looked at in greater depth
Either one or two specific subjects are taken and dealt with in depth, providing practical explanation and advice.

Questions and Answers
This section answers commonly raised questions. Subscribers are encouraged to write to *Team Leader's Briefing* with any questions on employment issues they may have.

Croner's Industrial Relations Law

An authoritative guide on all the legal provisions which regulate the relationship between employer and trade union members and trade unions.

Contents Include

The Parties to Industrial Relations
Employers and Trade Unions
Employers and Trade Union Members
Trade Unions and Trade Union Members
Further Information.

The Information Service Includes

- A loose-leaf reference guide
- Quarterly updates to the loose-leaf
- Monthly Industrial Relations Briefing
- Electronic disk version of the loose-leaf.

Croner's Employment Case Law Index

Structured to keep the busy personnel professional up to date and to locate relevant facts and summaries of findings for significant cases.

Contents Include

Contracts of Employment
Continuity of Employment
Employment Protection Rights
Disciplinary Procedures
Unfair Dismissal
Redundancy
Transfer of Undertakings
Sex Discrimination
Race Discrimination.

The Information Service Includes

- A loose-leaf reference guide
- Quarterly updates to the loose-leaf, including HotDocs interactive software
- Electronic disk version of the loose-leaf
- Monthly bulletins.

Croner's A–Z Guide for HRM Professionals

Providing information on a wide spectrum of human resource management and organisational issues to enable the identification, planning and implementation of a business-led HR strategy.

Contents Include

Career Management
Corporate Strategy
HRM Planning
Job Evaluation
Management
Marketing
Psychometric Tests
Quality Reward Management.

The Information Service Includes

- A loose-leaf reference guide
- Quarterly updates to the loose-leaf
- Electronic disk version of the loose-leaf
- Monthly HRM Professionals Briefing
- Quarterly 32 page *Journal of Professional HRM.*

Croner's Employment Law for Local Authority Employers

A practical guide for local authority personnel and line managers concentrating on all aspects of employment legislation specifically affecting local government, including special provisions and implications of major policy issues.

Contents Include

General Issues
Appointments and Contracts
Part-time, Temporary and Casual Employment
Pay Issues
Employment Protection
European Law
Equalities
Absence and Related Matters
Trade Unions
Health and Safety
Key Policy Issues.

The Information Service Includes

- A loose-leaf reference guide
- Quarterly updates to the loose-leaf
- Electronic disk version of the loose-leaf
- Fortnightly Local Authorities Briefing.

Croner's Employment Law Line

A telephone advisory service which is specially designed to provide guidance on difficult and individual employment-related problems.

The Information Service Includes

- Telephone advisory service
- Personnel in Practice loose-leaf reference service updated quarterly
- Electronic disk version of the loose-leaf, including HotDocs interactive software.
- Fortnightly Employment Digest
- Monthly Employment Case Digest.

Croner's Guide to Contracts of Employment

A practical guide to provide employers with information on the range of issues which frequently arise concerning the contractual nature of the employment relationship. The HotDocs software on the disk version of the loose-leaf enables you to customise contracts, clauses and letters.

Contents Include

The Employment Relationship
Components of the Contract
Implied Terms
Protecting Goodwill and Trade Secrets
Varying the Contract
Termination
Industrial Action
TUPE
Staff Handbooks.

The Information Service Includes

- A loose-leaf reference guide
- Two updates a year
- Monthly Employment Contracts Briefing
- Electronic disk version of the loose-leaf, which includes HotDocs software.

For further information, please contact our Customer Services Team on 0181-247 1176.

Index

D

E

F

G

H

I

L

M

N

O

P

R

S

T

U

V

W

Y